Critical Reasoning

A Romp through the Foothills of Logic for the Complete Beginner

Marianne Talbot

Table of Contents

Introduction

Have you ever wished you could argue more convincingly? Or perhaps you have always wanted to be able to evaluate the arguments of others more effectively? If you've ever been in either of these situations this book is for you. I have written it to help those who have never studied argument get to grips with the skills they need to argue, and evaluate others' arguments, effectively.

A careful reading of this book will enable you to:

- understand what an argument is;

- recognise arguments;

- analyse arguments;

- distinguish deductive arguments from inductive arguments;

- evaluate inductive and deductive arguments;

- understand formal and informal fallacies;

- understand the rudiments of formalisation;

- apply the rules of propositional logic.

I have added a chapter on formalisation and the rules of propositional logic for fun. I have found that people are often fascinated to see how (and why) logicians work with 'P's and 'Q's. You may be surprised at how easy it is (at least at the entry level where we'll be working). If you are one of those people who are 'allergic' to symbols (I have met only a few in my 30 years of teaching elementary logic at Oxford University) you can just skip the last two chapters.

I have written this book to complement my podcasts on critical reasoning. These were made available on iTunesU by Oxford University. You can access them here: www.philosophy.ox.ac.uk/ podcasts/critical_reasoning_for_beginners. For those who prefer to read, or who are hearing-impaired, there is a transcript for each podcast at mariannetalbot.co.uk/transcripts/.

The first series shot to number one in the iTunesU charts. On May 3rd 2011 it held every single one of the top ten download positions. It has been back to number one several times. I have had email from people all over the world saying they have enjoyed the podcasts. Many asked if I had written a book on critical reasoning.

Well, I have now. I am writing this as an e-book because doing so enables me to publish it at £5.99. Print-on-demand technology has also allowed it to be printed in paperback only slightly more expensively. As the cost of print books goes up (my last one was £60 in hardback!), I am delighted to publish a book that nearly everyone will be able to afford. Ideally you will read it having watched or listened to the podcasts, they are completely free and available in both audio and video. Links will appear to the relevant podcast as you reach the relevant part of the book. You can also find all my podcasts on my website: www.mariannetalbot.co.uk

I was very keen to write an e-book, so you might wonder why I am producing a hard copy. The main reason is that so many people asked for it. Not everyone is happy reading on an e-book, some people are unable to purchase the e-book and some people (and I have to admit I am amongst them) prefer to read academic books in hard copy. Anyway, if you are reading this in hard copy I hope you are glad that Chris Wood (who helped me put this book online and helped also to produce the hard copy) and I decided to go ahead!

There are two series of podcasts, corresponding to two series of lectures I gave at the Department for Continuing Education, the University of Oxford. The first is called 'Critical Reasoning', the second 'A Romp Through the Foothills of Logic'. It is the second series that grounds this book. Both sets of lectures were given to members of the public. I didn't assume any previous knowledge or understanding of logic. Many people were thinking about critical reasoning for the first time ever. I hope that these podcasts, in the context of this book, will help you to overcome any initial difficulties you might have.

I used this book as the required reading for an online course (https://www.conted.ox.ac.uk/courses/critical-reasoning-a-romp-through-the-foothills-of-logic-online) I wrote for Oxford University. Doing this course will enable you to learn how to reason critically in the company of others who are doing the same. You will also have the guidance of a tutor who will help you when things get difficult. The course includes activities to be done as individuals and as groups. If you learn better in company then the course is for you.

In writing this book I have had second thoughts about some of the things in the podcasts. I give plenty of warning of this so it won't confuse you. The biggest change is that I have reversed the order in which I have discussed the evaluation of inductive and deductive arguments. In the podcasts I did the latter first then the former. In the book I do the former first then the latter. The chapters on formalisation are covered in the second set of podcasts.

Using this book

This is not the sort of book that you can dip into. Each chapter introduces a new set of skills and each set builds on the skills introduced in previous chapters. You will get the most out of the book if you start at chapter one and continue until at least chapter six. Chapters seven and eight can be skipped by anyone who isn't interested in formalising arguments. There are exercises throughout the book. Answers are provided to all the exercises in appendix IV at the back of the book. Sometimes it will be suggested that any difficulties you are having might be alleviated by watching one of the podcasts. There are also truth table definitions and tableaux rules in appendices II and III to assist with the exercises in chapters seven and eight. Words that have precise meanings in the context of Critical Reasoning have definitions in the book where they are first mentioned; these definitions are collated in appendix I.

A Note to Instructors

I know that many teachers are using the podcasts to introduce critical reasoning to their students. Many have contacted me to ask for permission. I am always happy to give permission so long as the podcasts are to be used for educational purposes. In fact if you are using them for educational purposes you do not even need to ask for permission; I have made all of them freely available on a 'creative commons licence'. This licence relinquishes my right to payment for the use of the podcasts unless they are to be used commercially. Should you want to make money from the podcasts please be in touch. For this you *do* need my permission.

In addition to the e-book and the podcasts, I also have:

a website: www.mariannetalbot.co.uk
a twitter feed: @oxphil_marianne
a Facebook page: Marianne Talbot Philosophy

Please come to visit me either by attending classes in Oxford, on my website or by email (there is a 'contact' form on my website) If you are enjoying the book I would love to hear about it. If you are not enjoying the book, tell me why. If you find something wrong with the book I would be particularly grateful if you'd let me know so I can make the appropriate changes.

Good luck in your studies!
Marianne Talbot
University of Oxford

August 2014

About the Author

Marianne Talbot was thrown out of school at 15 for truancy and disruption. Having dabbled in sales and marketing for a couple of years she spent the next five years travelling in Europe, Asia, the Antipodes and Africa. At 26, back in Britain and starved of intellectual stimulation, she started a Foundation Course with the Open University. During this she discovered philosophy (specifically logic). Having found what she wanted to do, she applied to London University and despite not having two 'O' levels to rub together she was admitted. Three years later she left, with a First Class degree, to do graduate work at Oxford.

Marianne has now been in Oxford for 30 years. She taught first at Pembroke College (1987 – 1990), then at Brasenose (1991- 2000). In 2001 she took up her current position as Director of Studies at the Department for Continuing Education, where she organises the university's 'outreach' in philosophy. She was responsible for pioneering Oxford's extremely popular online short courses in philosophy, and has written four of them herself, including the one on critical reasoning. Marianne's job makes her automatically President of the OUDCE Philosophical Society. This currently has nearly 400 members, many from overseas, and a very comprehensive website: www.oxfordphilsoc.org.uk

From 1996-2000 Marianne chaired the National Forum for Values in Education and the Community. This group was responsible for writing the statement of values that underpins the National Curriculum in England. In this capacity Marianne was responsible, under the Qualifications and Curriculum Authority, for promoting the spiritual, moral, social and cultural development of English pupils from 5-19. She was also a member of several governmental advisory groups including the Cabinet Office's group on Vision and Values, and the Advisory Group for Citizenship and Democracy in Schools. The latter was responsible for introducing Citizenship into the National Curriculum.

Marianne teaches research ethics, philosophy of science and subject-area ethics for several of the doctoral training centres funded by the Engineering and Physical Sciences Research Council. From 2001-2007 she was a Trustee of the Girls' Day School Trust.

Both Marianne's parents had dementia. She cared for them for 13 years. For 5 of these her Mum lived with her. These years are chronicled in the book *Keeping Mum: Caring for Someone with Dementia*. 5% of Marianne's profits from this book go to Alzheimer's Research UK, for whom Marianne is a 'National Champion'. Marianne is also a National Ambassador for Carers' UK and a Carers' Champion for Age UK Oxfordshire.

Marianne loves to walk, especially in the Lake District, Dartmoor and the Cambrian Mountains.

Acknowledgements

Many people have been hugely helpful in helping me get this, my first e-book, to the stage of being published. They have proof-read, edited, peer-reviewed or helped me with the technical stuff. I really appreciate their help. Here are their names:

Dr. Sophie Allen
Dr. Paula Boddington
John Clare
Dr.Lyndon Entwhistle
Dr. Andrew Hull
Dominic La Hausse de Lalouvière
Dr. Stephen Law
Dr. Andrea Lechler
Dr. Rachel Paine
Steve Pierce
Dr. Brian Prince
Bill Radcliffe
Chris Reason
Peter Robinson
Chris Wood

The podcasts used in chapters 7 and 8, and the slides and transcripts for all the podcasts are used with the kind permission of Oxford University's Department for Continuing Education, in particular the kind folks at TALL (Technology Assisted Lifelong Learning). If I have forgotten anyone, please let me know and I shall make sure your name is added asap!

Naturally if there are any errors they are all mine. I should be very grateful if you would let me know if you find any.

CHAPTER ONE

The Nature of Argument

This chapter corresponds to the first podcast in my series: **Critical Reasoning: A Romp Through the Foothills of Logic** available in both audio (metafore.com/CR1audio) and video (metafore.com/CR1video) with accompanying slides (metafore.com/CR1slides) and transcripts (http://mariannetalbot.co.uk/transcripts/).

Listening to the podcasts either before, or after, you read the chapter will help you with any difficulties you might have.

To study critical reasoning is to study *arguments* and the *sentences* that constitute them. It is to look at the rational relations between the beliefs that are expressed in the sentences that constitute the arguments you use, and it is to learn how to evaluate arguments as *good* or *bad*.

We shall not be considering how to evaluate arguments in this chapter. Before we can get to that we shall be considering how to recognise arguments, how to analyse them and how to classify them. We shall only start to evaluate arguments in chapter four. It'll be worth the wait because, by that time, you will have learned a great deal about arguments, and you will have acquired the concepts and distinctions you need when evaluating arguments in a rigorous and productive way.

In this chapter we shall be considering the nature of an argument. You will discover that an argument is a set of sentences that are rationally related to each other in a very particular way.

By the time you have finished this chapter you will be able to:

- recognise arguments, sentences and assertions;

- distinguish between simple and complex sentences;

- know when a complex sentence can be said to be an argument;

- distinguish between *using* a sentence and *mentioning* that sentence;

- recognise and test for declarative sentences;

- distinguish weak and strong meaning;

- distinguish between truth values and truth conditions;

- explain the importance of arguing in accordance with the Principle of Charity.

At the end of the chapter we will pause for you to reflect on whether you can indeed do these things.

But we've got some work to do. So let's get started.

Good luck!

Recognising Arguments

You might think it is easy to recognise arguments. But the word 'argument' in English has more than one meaning; it is *ambiguous*. In chapter two we shall discuss ambiguity in some depth. In this chapter it is important only for you to be able to recognise arguments.

In the podcast (slides 4-12) I used the Monty Python sketch "The Argument Clinic" (metafore.com/cr/arg) to prompt discussion of two definitions of 'argument'. The first definition was given by 'A' who said:

"An argument is a connected series of statements to establish a
   definite proposition."

This definition is rejected by 'M' who counters:

"If I argue with you, I must take up a contrary position."

Consider the difference between arguing *for* something, and arguing *with* someone. One of these definitions suits the former, the other the latter

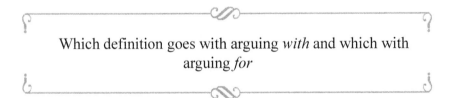

Which definition goes with arguing *with* and which with
arguing *for*

M's definition defines 'argument' in the context of arguing *with* someone. A, on the other hand, defines 'argument' in the context of arguing *for* something. When we argue *with* someone, of course, we are usually arguing *for* something. It is not always the case, though, that when we argue *for* something we are arguing *with* someone. We may simply be trying to convince them of something. We may even be trying to convince *ourselves* of something.

In studying critical reasoning we are primarily interested in arguing *for* something rather than arguing *with* someone. The definition of 'argument' we'll use in this book reflects that.

This is the definition of 'argument' we'll use in this book:

Def: an *argument* **is a set of sentences in which one sentence is being asserted on the basis of the other(s).**

We shall not neglect the other sort of argument. Later in this chapter we shall look at the best way to go about arguing *with* someone.

You'll note that I talk about 'sentences' whilst the Monty Python definition talks of 'statements'. I shall be explaining in later chapters the difference between a statement and a sentence. I have chosen to define arguments in terms of sentences because it is an easier concept for a beginner to grasp.

To understand our definition of 'argument' clearly we need to understand exactly what is meant by *sentence,* and we need to know what it is for a sentence to be *asserted.* We also need to know what a *set* of sentences is, and what it is to assert one sentence *on the basis* of others. In this chapter we shall look at all these things.

We shall also look at the nature of beliefs as *reasons* for thinking, doing and saying something, at the difference between using and mentioning sentences and arguments, and at the difference between weak and strong meanings, and truth values and truth conditions.

But first: what is a sentence?

Sentences

Most of us are capable of recognising a sentence, even if we are not sure how to explain what it is. So you are probably aware that sentences start with capital letters, end with full stops, and that there are two sentences in this paragraph (including this one).

Sentences, however, are extremely important when studying critical reasoning, so let's reflect for a moment on the nature of a sentence. We can start by noting that a sentence is a group of words that is *complete in itself* as the expression of a thought.

Imagine that you and a friend are discussing a film you've just seen and your friend says to you 'The film...'

Your friend hasn't said anything yet, has she? You are left waiting for her to finish her sentence. You can guess she is probably talking about the film you have just seen, but until she *predicates* something of the film, until she attributes some property to it, you haven't learned anything about what she thinks about it.

If, on the other hand, she says 'The film was fantastic!' now she has expressed a complete thought by uttering a complete sentence. She has identified both what it is she is talking about and what she is saying about it. You now know that she thinks the film was fantastic. (We shall assume throughout this book that anyone expressing a belief is expressing it sincerely.)

In uttering a complete sentence, a sentence with a *subject* (an expression identifying what she is talking about) and a *predicate* (an expression identifying what she is saying about the subject), your friend has expressed a belief. You can tell it is a belief because she has uttered something with a *truth value*. It is either true or false.

> **Def:** we attach a *truth value* to a sentence (or the belief it expresses) when we say it is true or we say it is false.

Usually your recognition that the sentence uttered by someone is either true or false will consist in your agreeing or disagreeing with it. To agree with a sentence as uttered by another person is to accept that sentence, and the belief it expresses, as *true*. To disagree with it is to reject it, and the belief it expresses, as *false*. (In this particular case the belief may be true for her and false for you).

Only sentences capable of expressing beliefs and beliefs capable of being expressed by sentences can be true or false. If there were no beliefs and no sentences capable of expressing beliefs, then there would be no truth or falsehood.

Truth and Falsehood

Arguments, for example, are not true or false. Arguments are only good or bad. So the sentences that *constitute* an argument – the sentence that is asserted, and those sentences on the basis of which the first is asserted – can all be true or false. But the argument itself cannot be true *or* false.

To say that an argument is true is to say something like 'that table is loud'. Such a sentence doesn't really make sense, as anyone who understands 'table' and 'loud' knows. To say 'that argument is true' is to say something equally meaningless.

Similarly, facts, events, and states of affairs are not true or false. It is this sort of thing that *makes* a sentence, and the belief it expresses, true or false. But this sort of thing is not *itself* true or false.

For example, the cat's being on the mat is a state of affairs. Philosophers would say that this state of affairs either *obtains* or it doesn't *obtain*. If it does obtain (if the cat *is* on the mat) then its obtaining will make the sentence 'the cat is on the mat' (and the belief expressed by that sentence) true. If it doesn't obtain (if the cat isn't on the mat) then its not obtaining will make the same sentence (and the same belief) false. If it doesn't obtain, of course, this will make the sentence 'the cat is *not* on the mat' (and the belief expressed by *that* sentence) true.

Importantly the state of affairs is not *itself* true or false. The cat's being on the mat is simply not the sort of thing that can be true or false. Just as someone sincerely attributing loudness to a table manifests his failure to understand 'table' and/or 'loud', someone who thinks of a state of affairs as *true* is one who manifests his misunderstanding of what a state of affairs is, and/or what the word 'true' means.

> *It is worth taking a moment to reflect on the last five paragraphs and make sure you understand them because sentences, beliefs and truth values are all very important in critical reasoning.*

Most sentences and beliefs have truth values. They are either true or false. It is a tenet of classical logic that there is no third truth value. According to classical logic there are also no truth value gaps. You will see below, though, that it is only when we *use* sentences that they have truth values.

Not everyone accepts classical logic. But the critical reasoning you are learning is based on classical logic, so we will accept its tenets. This means accepting *bivalence* (the belief that when a sentence has a truth value it will be either true or it will be false). We'll see later that *every* sentence, when it is being used, has a truth value.

> *Take a moment to make sure you have understood bivalence. Although we shall be accepting it for the purposes of this book we should recognise that some philosophers reject classical logic because they reject bivalence. Ask yourself whether 'the dress is red' is always either true or false, or whether 'the dress is not not red' (for example) suggests otherwise. If you would like to read more about this try: An Introduction to Non-Classical Logic From If to Is, by Graham Priest, Cambridge University Press, ISBN: 9780521670265 You can find it here: http://www.st-andrews.ac.uk/philosophy/old/gp /gp.html*

Assertions

Your friend believes that the sentence she uttered, 'this film is fantastic!', is true. We know this because she asserted it (and we are assuming she asserted it sincerely). To assert a sentence sincerely is to use it to express a belief. Your friend therefore *believes* the film was fantastic, and she is expressing that belief in her assertion 'the film was fantastic'.

Let's look more closely at assertions.

Language is a tool. By means of it we communicate with others, informing them about the world, our thoughts and emotions, and everything else that strikes us as interesting, important or useful. We can also ask questions, discovering from others how they see or feel about the world. Sometimes we issue commands, prompting others to change the world. At other times we issue warnings and reassurances. Nearly all interactions between human beings are mediated by language.

It is by the *force* we use when we utter a sentence that we indicate what it is we are doing with the sentence. When we express a belief we utter a sentence with *assertoric force* ('The film was fantastic'). To do this is to make an assertion. If we were to utter the same sentence with *interrogative force* we would be asking a question ('Was the film fantastic?'). If, on the other hand, we uttered it with *imperative force*, we would be issuing a command ('Make the film fantastic!').

In studying critical reasoning, we are mainly interested in sentences uttered with assertoric force because these are sentences that are being used to express beliefs, sentences with *truth values*. Commands don't have truth values. Neither do questions. Assertions, however, do have truth values: they can be either true or false.

> **Def:** an *assertion* is a sentence used with assertoric force to express a belief.

The use of language to express beliefs is particularly important in the study of critical reasoning because, as we'll see in the next section, beliefs are themselves important to critical reasoning.

Beliefs and Reasons

It is important to understand that in discussing beliefs we are not discussing *religious* beliefs. We are talking about the beliefs that constitute our *reasons* for thinking what we think, doing what we do, and saying what we say. Many of these beliefs are everyday beliefs. Some are scientific and some are indeed religious.

Human beings form beliefs about the world all the time. Some of these beliefs are about our immediate environment, for example [my cup of coffee is to my right] or [I am in front of the computer], others are about abstract states of affairs like [no matter travels faster than the speed of light] or [2+2=4]. (The square brackets indicate beliefs.)

Our beliefs, together with our desires, drive us round the world. You do whatever you do because you are motivated by your desires and guided towards your goal by your beliefs.

We have many beliefs of which we are unaware. Have you ever noticed, for example, that you believe that zebras don't carry handbags? You probably haven't. But if asked whether zebras carry handbags, you would say 'no' pretty quickly.

It may be incorrect to say you already believed zebras don't carry handbags before you read the last four sentences. Perhaps reading these sentences brought your belief into existence? Certainly, though, the belief that zebras don't carry handbags is a logical consequence of beliefs you *did* have. You would have seen this the minute you considered the question.
Generally speaking you are good at working out the logical consequences of your beliefs. You are also, generally speaking, quite good at working out what you need to do to satisfy your desires. This is because you are rational. Being rational you are sensitive to the rational relations between your beliefs. It is because of the beliefs you have and the rational relations between them that you do, believe and say whatever you do, believe or say.

In studying critical reasoning it is your beliefs, the rational relations between them, and the sentences that express them, that we'll be studying.

Sets of Sentences

Look again at the definition of 'argument':

Def: **an *argument* is a set of sentences in which one sentence is asserted on the basis of the other(s).**

So far we have considered the nature of sentences as expressing complete thoughts; beliefs with a truth value. We have also looked at the fact that when we assert a sentence we express a belief, and at the fact that beliefs are often *reasons* for further beliefs and, together with desires, reasons for action. Now let's look at the fact that an argument is a *set of* sentences.

No *single* sentence can constitute an argument. This is because an argument essentially involves two things:

1 the assertion of a sentence expressing a belief

2 the giving of reasons to support that belief

If all we do is express a belief we are not making an argument. An argument essentially involves the assertion of a sentence together with (a set of) *reasons* for holding the belief expressed by that sentence. Assertions are not, on their own, arguments, as you'll have realised if you watched podcast one (note especially the 'argument' between Lin and Jim on slide 21).

So every argument involves an assertion which we call the *conclusion*, and at least one reason for holding the belief expressed by that assertion, at least one *premise*. The conclusion of the argument is the assertion which expresses the belief for which an argument is being made. The premise(s) of the argument are the reason(s) being offered for the conclusion.

> **Def:** the *conclusion* of an argument is the assertion being made on the basis of the other sentences.

> **Def:** the *premise (s)* of an argument are the reason(s) being offered for believing the conclusion.

Simple Versus Complex Sentences

It is immediately necessary to clarify the claim that no argument can consist in a single sentence. This is because a moment's thought will make it obvious there are arguments constituted of single sentences. Here is one:

(1) The mail is always late when it rains so, as it is raining, the mail will be late.

This complication demonstrates only that we need to distinguish between *complex* sentences and *simple* sentences. The difference is that a complex sentence is itself constituted of sentences – it has sentences as *parts*. A simple sentence is such that all its parts are *sub-sentential*. So if a sentence is such that none of its parts are themselves sentences it is a simple sentence. The sentence 'the cat is on the mat' is a simple sentence.

The sentence above, labelled (1), is a complex sentence. We can tell this because it can be analysed into parts that are themselves sentences (and logical words or 'sentence connectives' such as 'and' or 'or'). It is (partly) because it is a complex sentence that it can be an argument.

Try identifying the sentences that together constitute the
complex sentence (1) before you read on to find the
answer.

Sentence (1) is not an argument *solely* because it can be analysed
into a set of simple sentences. It is also an argument because one
of the simple sentences is being asserted (is playing the role of a
conclusion), and the others are being offered as reasons for
believing that one (are playing the role of premises). Both these
conditions must be satisfied for a complex sentence to be an
argument.

Try identifying the sentence that is being asserted (the
conclusion) and those on the basis of which the assertion is
being made (the premises) before you read on to find the
answer.

The assertion being made in sentence (1) is that the mail will be
late. The reasons that are offered for this assertion are firstly that
the mail is always late when it rains, and secondly that it is
raining. The fact we can analyse this complex sentence into a set
of simple sentences one of which is being asserted on the basis of
the others, means that this complex sentence is, in fact, an
argument even though it is only one sentence.

To be precise, therefore, we should claim that no single *simple*
sentence can be an argument.

It is important to note that complex sentences are arguments only if they can be analysed into simple sentences such that one is being asserted on the basis of the others. There are complex sentences of which this is not true. Consider, for example, the sentence:

> (2) If she is a professional soprano then she should be able to reach top A.

This complex sentence *isn't* analysable into an argument. Can you say why before you read on to find my answer?

This sentence is certainly constituted of two simple sentences ('she is a professional soprano' and 'she should be able to reach top A') and the logical words 'if/then'. But anyone using this sentence would not be asserting either of these sentences on the basis of the other. One using this sentence is neither claiming that she *is* a professional soprano *or* that she can reach top A. Instead they are asserting the whole complex conditional. They are claiming only that *if* she is a professional soprano she should be able to reach top A. The constituent sentences are not separable into one that is being asserted, and the other offered as a reason for the assertion.

This sentence, therefore, cannot be analysed into a set of sentences that satisfies our definition of argument. It can be analysed into simple sentences, but these sentences are not related in the right way for an argument. A complex sentence must meet both conditions before it can be said to be an argument. Make sure you understand this before you read on.

Exercise 1.1: Which of the following sets of sentences are arguments? Remember that a set of sentences is an argument only if one sentence is being asserted on the basis of the others.

1.   As she got nearer home, her worry increased and she quickened her step. Then, just before she put her key in the front door her mobile rang.

2.   Since Jennifer is the mother of Stan, and Stan is the father of Oliver, Jennifer is the grandmother of Oliver.

3.   The Challenger exploded because the O-rings failed, and the proper functioning of the O-rings was a necessary part of a safe launch.

4.   Justin Beiber was late, and many of his fans were upset. The twittersphere was very busy.

5.   If the train was held up Jem will be late.

6.   The small bird was a robin, the large one a woodpecker.

7.   If the car is not starting you might think about calling the AA.

Answers on page 349

Use and Mention

We are now going to consider another complication. In studying critical reasoning we will be *using* many sentences and many arguments. We will also be *talking about* many sentences and many arguments.

Language has an existence independently of its being used. In talking about language we recognise this. It is not possible, of course, to talk about language except by using language. We need, therefore, a way of indicating when a bit of language is being mentioned rather than used. In everyday life we use quotation marks.

If, for example, we put quotation marks around the sentence 'the cat is on the mat' we can now talk *about* this sentence. The sentence is now being used to refer to *itself*, not to talk about cats and mats. We can now say, for example, that the sentence has 6 words, and that it is partly constituted of the words 'cat' and 'mat'. If we put quotes around the word 'cat', furthermore, we can meaningfully say of it that it has three letters. This is not something we can meaningfully say of any *cat*.

The effect of the quotation marks around 'the cat is on the mat' is to indicate that we are not *using* the sentence to talk about a cat's being on a mat, nor are we expressing a belief that the cat is on the mat, we are simply *mentioning* a sentence that could be used in various ways, not least to express the belief that the cat is on the mat.

Declarative Sentences

A sentence that *could* be used with assertoric force to express a belief is called a 'declarative sentence':

Def: a *declarative sentence* **is a sentence that could be used with assertoric force to express a belief.**

We shall be using a lot of declarative sentences in this book. It is important, therefore, that you be able to recognise them. The test for a declarative sentence is whether it can be substituted for '…' in the question 'Is it true that …?' to yield a grammatical question. This is called the 'frame test'

For example we know 'the cat is on the mat' is a declarative sentence because if we substitute it for '…' in 'Is it true that…?' we get 'Is it true that the cat is on the mat?' which is a grammatical question.

Although we shall be using declarative sentences a lot in this book we shan't always be putting them in quotation marks. If we did it would look very messy. In the next chapter, for example, we shall be learning how to analyse arguments and set them out logic-book style. Here is the argument we discussed above set out logic-book style:

Premise one: The mail is always late when it rains

Premise two: It is raining

Conclusion: The mail will be late.

Each of the sentences constituting this argument is a declarative sentence (use the frame test to check that this is the case). Each of them is a sentence that *could* be used to make an assertion and so express a belief. The fact that the final sentence is labelled 'conclusion' marks the fact that if the argument were being *used* rather than mentioned, this is the sentence that would be being asserted on the basis of the others.

I hope you'll agree that (a) putting quotation marks around these sentences would look messy, (b) the fact they are declarative sentences is clear without the quotation marks, and (c) that it is also clear that it is the sentence labeled 'conclusion' that would be being asserted on the basis of the others (labeled 'premises one and two') if the argument were being used.

Exercise 1.2: Recognising Declarative Sentences.
Use the frame test to decide whether the following are declarative sentences:

1. The snow is still falling.

2. Inflation is slowly rising.

3. Is it time yet?

4. I hereby declare you man and wife.

5. Has the shopping arrived yet?

6. Turn that noise off!

7. I hope you feel better.

Answers on page 351

Truth Conditions and Truth Values

The distinction between *using* sentences and arguments, and *talking about* (or *mentioning)* sentences and arguments is important. One reason it is important is because sentences in use have truth values. Sentences that are merely being mentioned (used to refer to themselves) are not usually thought of as having truth values.

We noted above that if someone asserts a sentence, thereby using it to express a belief, their assertion will be either true or false; it will have a truth value. But if a teacher writes on the board a sentence like 'James is very tall' in order to discuss its subject/predicate form, the sentence written on the board, a declarative sentence, is neither true nor false. No-one is asserting, of any James, that he is very tall. No belief is being expressed. We are merely talking about a sentence that *could be used* to assert, of someone called 'James', that he is very tall. A declarative sentence (a sentence that is being *talked about*) is neither true nor false (though it is difficult not to think of sentences like 'grass is green' as having a truth value).

Although declarative sentences do not have truth values, they do have *truth conditions.* The truth conditions of a sentence are those conditions under which the sentence *would* be true or false if used with its 'strict and literal' meaning, the meaning that would, under normal conditions, be assigned to the sentence by one who speaks the language.

> **Def:** ***Truth conditions* are those conditions under which a sentence would be true or false if it were used under normal conditions to express a belief (the strict and literal meaning of a sentence is given by its truth conditions).**

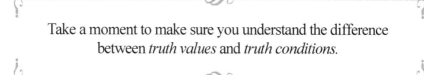

Take a moment to make sure you understand the difference
between *truth values* and *truth conditions.*

It is in virtue of grasping the truth conditions of the sentence
'James is very tall' that we would claim to understand the sentence
the teacher writes on the board. To grasp the truth conditions of
this sentence is to grasp its strict and literal meaning.

In fact, though, we only understand the sentence in a very weak
sense. This is because the sentence only has *meaning* in a very
weak sense. It has meaning *only* in virtue of being associated with
a strict and literal meaning, a set of truth conditions. A sentence
that is being used, rather than merely mentioned, has meaning in a
much stronger sense: the fact it is being used means that the
sentence is uttered in a context that, with luck, will enable one
who grasps its truth conditions to determine its truth value in that
context, because they can identify the belief the sentence is being
used to express.

In this book we shall occasionally talk as if declarative sentences
have truth values. When we do this, however, it will be because
we are imagining that the declarative sentences *are* being used in a
context to make an assertion.

Weak and Strong Meaning

So imagine that instead of simply mentioning the sentence 'James is very tall', Sara asserts this sentence to express the belief [James is very tall] to her friends Deepak and Jem, both of whom know James. Deepak and Jem, both of whom grasp the truth conditions of the sentence (its *weak* meaning), will be in a position to see immediately whether or not the sentence Sara has asserted is true.

In virtue of their grasp of the truth conditions of the sentence, they are able to make use of these truth conditions – their knowledge of the identity of James, and their understanding of what it is to be very tall – to determine whether or not this particular assertion of 'James is very tall' (and the belief expressed by it) is true or false.

Determining truth and falsity is always a matter of combining (a) knowledge of meaning, and (b) knowledge of the world.

The very same sentence might, of course, in one context be true and in another context false. Some men called 'James' *are* very tall, others arcn't.

The *strong* meaning of a sentence is the meaning it has when it is being used, with a particular force in a particular context, to express a belief. As we'll see below assertions with the same *weak* meaning may differ with respect to their *strong* meanings. This is because one and the same declarative sentence can be used to make different assertions.

This distinction between *weak meaning* and *strong meaning*, between the strict and literal meaning had by a declarative sentence, and the meaning of the same sentence as used in a given context, is hugely important. Our grasp of this distinction, even without our realising that we grasp it, is part of what enables us to do things with sentences *other* than use them with their strict and literal meanings.

The Flexibility of Language

Imagine, for example, that you have just asked Sara whether James is a good philosopher. Further imagine that, having definitely heard and understood your question, Sara replies, perhaps in an odd sort of voice: 'James is very tall'.

Has Sara answered your question? If so what was her answer?

You probably believe that Sara *has* answered your question, and that her answer was that she *doesn't* think James is a good philosopher. Sara was using the sentence 'James is very tall', in this particular context, to express her belief that James is not a good philosopher. It is the belief Sara expressed by her utterance, in the context in which she made the utterance, that constitutes the strong meaning of the sentence she used.

This means that a sentence with the *weak* meaning 'James is very tall' can, in a particular context, have the strong meaning 'James is not a good philosopher'. You might reasonably think it is a wonder we ever understand anything at all!

There are, though, clues to the (strong) meaning of Sara's utterance that any normal adult speaker of English will pick up. Probably the most important one is that the *weak* meaning of Sara's utterance, given how inappropriate it is in the context, is probably *not* the meaning that Sara intended to convey. Recognising this you would immediately be alert for the meaning Sara *did* intend; for the *strong* meaning of Sara's utterance, for the belief she is *in fact* expressing.

Knowing that Sara's utterance was intended as an answer to your question, you would probably bring to bear a bit of psychology. Recognising that Sara might be reluctant to say outright that she doesn't think James is a good philosopher, you would probably hypothesise that Sara has chosen to *imply* this by uttering, as an answer to the question, a sentence the strict and literal truth conditions of which were totally inappropriate. In doing this Sara hopes that you would be able to work out her true meaning (the *strong* meaning of her utterance): that she is expressing the belief that James is not a good philosopher. We can *imply* something by intentionally using words the strict and literal meanings of which arc not entirely appropriate to the context in which we use the words.

Even though the strong meaning of Sara's utterance was quite different from its weak meaning, you would not have been able to work out the strong meaning without knowing the weak meaning. It was your grasp of the weak meaning, plus your understanding of the context and a bit of psychology, that enabled you to work out the strong meaning of Sara's utterance. Even if a sentence is not used with its strict and literal meaning, therefore, we still need to understand this meaning to work out the strong meaning of a sentence – what it is being *used* to mean.

The Tone of Utterance

There is one final element to the use of language we need to discuss: the tone with which we utter our words. We mentioned above that Sara might have uttered the words 'James is very tall' in an odd sort of voice. This, the tone with which she uttered the sentence, might have been one of your clues to the strong meaning of her sentence.

Now imagine that Sara and James are having a serious row, and James says to Sara in an accusing tone "you're angry!" Imagine that Sara's response is to scream at James "I am *not* angry!"

I think you'll agree that Sara's tone gives her away. She is saying she is not angry (i.e. this is the weak meaning of the sentence she uses), but in such tone of voice that we won't believe her. Her tone contradicts the strict and literal meaning of her words. If she does believe she is not angry she is deluding herself.

Another tone we might use is sarcasm. Imagine that Sergei has turned up late to every single one of the nine classes you have attended this term. We are ten minutes into the tenth class, the door slams back and Sergei rushes in. The teacher says sarcastically "Early again Sergei". The teacher has *not* said Sergei is early again, has he? The effect of his sarcastic tone, together with the context in which he makes his utterance, has the effect of making the strong meaning of his utterance exactly the opposite of its weak meaning.

Normal speakers of a language are very good indeed at working out the strong meaning of an utterance from its weak meaning and clues of force, tone and context. In this book we shall mainly be dealing in weak meanings, but sometimes you will come across an exercise that expects you to *imagine* that someone is uttering certain words and to work out from these words the strong meaning of these words; the belief that person is expressing.

Imagine, for example, that someone utters the following sentence:

(3) If that's gold I am a Dutchman.

Which belief, do you think, is being expressed by that person? Which sentence would have the right *weak* meaning to express the *strong* meaning of the words uttered by one using sentence (3)?

Anyone familiar with the idiom will, of course, say the person is expressing the belief that whatever is being talked about is *not* gold. The strong meaning of the sentence used is expressed by the declarative sentence 'That is *not* gold'.

Exercise 1.3: Weak and Strong Meanings:

Imagine that someone utters the following sentences, then work out the declarative sentence that has the right *weak* meaning to express the *strong* meaning of that use of the sentence:

1. If Britain still has its triple A rating by the end of the year then the moon is made of green cheese

2. You wish you could earn more money? If wishes were horses beggars would ride.

3. He says he's a millionaire but you can tell that to the marines.

Answers on page 352

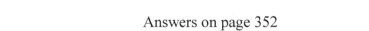

We have now covered everything we are going to cover in this chapter about how to recognise arguments *for* something. But I said that before we finished we would learn something about arguing *with* someone.

The Principle of Charity

Here is the philosopher Donald Davidson talking about what we do (or should do) when we try to understand another person:

"In our need to make him make sense we will try for a theory that finds him consistent, a believer of truths, and a lover of the good (all by our own lights it goes without saying)."[1]

The 'theory' Davidson is talking about here is the theory (or *interpretation*) you construct as you try to understand another person. So, as you observe their behaviour and listen to them talk, you decide that they *believe* certain things, that they *want* certain things, that they *like* and *dislike* certain things and so on. Every time they move or speak you will be able to add to your theory about their mental states (your *interpretation* of them) until, when you know them very well, you will often be able successfully to predict what they will say or do next.

Donald Davidson who died in 2003, was one of the most influential philosophers of the 20th century, you can read the Stanford Encyclopaedia entry on him here: metafore.com/cr/davidson

---

[1] (p. 222 'Mental Events', in Davidson's Essays on Actions and Events, also available free here: metafore.com/cr/davidson2)

Davidson is suggesting that when you first start trying to understand someone, if your interpretation portrays them as evil, inconsistent and/or a believer of falsehoods then you should at least consider the possibility that you have misunderstood them.

Davidson wasn't naïve. He knew that some people *are* evil, all of us are occasionally inconsistent and we all have *some* false beliefs.

But he firmly believed that, because we are rational, most people are such that, most of the time, most of the beliefs they have are true and consistent, and most of their desires benign. He argued that it is a necessary condition of our successfully understanding others that we start by assuming they are rational and that most of their beliefs are consistent and true. He also argued that anyone *all* of whose beliefs were false would be completely uninterpretable.

But was Davidson right? And what implications does this have for the study of critical reasoning?

Understanding Each Other

Imagine that Jem says: 'Marianne is wearing jeans and a skirt' You might immediately think that the belief Jem seems to be expressing is rather odd. Why would Marianne be wearing jeans *and* a skirt? Your next thought might be something like 'but if he doesn't mean what he seems to mean, what *does* he mean?'

Your failure to understand him isn't a failure to understand the words that he uttered. The sentence Jem uttered is not *linguistically* odd. What is odd is that anyone would wear both a skirt and jeans. Accordingly Charity exhorts us to hesitate before attributing to Jem the belief that someone *is* wearing both jeans and a skirt. Attributing to Jem the belief he seems to be expressing means attributing to him a belief that appears to be *false*.

If, as Davidson says, we must approach interpretation on the assumption that most people, most of the time, are rational, good and their beliefs mainly true, then attributing beliefs that suggest our subject is irrational, bad or in possession of false beliefs, smacks of inconsistency. In this appearance of inconsistency we have evidence for *error*. This is why we should hesitate: error is *bad!*

What we don't know, though, is where the error lies. It could be that Jem *does* have a false belief about what Marianne is wearing. But it could also be that there is something wrong with your interpretation of Jem: perhaps you are wrong to think he said what you think he said, or meant what you think he meant?

Asking for Explanations

The sensible thing to do is to *ask* Jem what he said, or what he meant, thereby giving Jem the opportunity either to correct your belief about what he said, or to explain what he means. You're most likely to get an illuminating answer if, when you ask him, you imply *you* might have misheard or misunderstood him, rather than that *he* is saying something odd.

Let's imagine that, in answer to your question, Jem says: 'I don't understand. What's odd about saying 'Marianne is wearing jeans and a shirt'? You thereby learn that you misheard the sentence Jem uttered.

Or let's imagine Jem says 'It *is* odd isn't it? I asked her why and she told me that she is cycling to a party, and doesn't want to ruin her skirt, so she is wearing her jeans under her skirt. When she gets to the party she will take off the jeans'. Once again, however odd *Marianne's behaviour* may seem, the oddness of Jem's utterance disappears. Now you know his *reason* for uttering his sentence you can see what he means.

Or Jem might say 'is that really what I said?! I should have said 'jeans and a *shirt*'. If this is the case you have allowed Jem to correct the mistake he made.

Now we can see why Charity is important. If, having decided Jem's belief was odd, you had taken this at face value and dismissed Jem as odd, you might have missed the opportunity to learn that the error was *your own*; that you had misheard him, or that you were wrong to assume that no-one could have good reason to believe that someone was wearing jeans *and* a skirt. Alternatively you may have missed the opportunity to help Jem correct his own error, for which he will surely be grateful, especially as you did it nicely; i.e. by wondering whether *you* were wrong, rather than assuming *he* was wrong.

If, in argument, you take care *always* to exercise the Principle of Charity you will be maximising your chances both of understanding others correctly, *and* of correcting, extending and confirming your own beliefs. If something someone says (or writes) strikes you as odd, false or wicked *always* check first that you have heard (or read) them correctly and if what they say still seems odd, false or wicked ask them their *reasons* for saying it.

If you do it nicely, implying that the error is probably *yours,* you will find that your arguments are far more productive. Certainly they will be more productive than they would have been if you had:

1. tried to correct the other (implying that the error is theirs);

2. allowed the apparent disagreement to pass in silence (because you were afraid to imply that a mistake was being made);

3. allowed the disagreement to pass in silence because you dismissed the person you were arguing with as irrational or stupid.

The Principle of Charity is so-called because it requires us to be *charitable* to others and to ourselves. So we should never offhandedly dismiss what others say as false or irrational, even if it seems that way to us. Nor should we automatically assume we are wrong when someone else thinks differently. To use the Principle of Charity is to recognise at all times that we may *ourselves* be wrong, either about our interpretation of another, or in our beliefs about the world. But it also reminds us that we might be *right* even if others disagree with us.

Pause for Reflection

At the beginning of this chapter I said that by the end of part one you would be able to:

- recognise arguments, sentences and assertions;

- distinguish between simple and complex sentences;

- know when a complex sentence can be said to be an argument;

- distinguish between using a sentence and mentioning that sentence;

- recognise and test for declarative sentences;

- distinguish weak and strong meaning;

- distinguish between truth values and truth conditions;

- argue in accordance with the Principle of Charity.

Can you do these things? Spend some time jotting down how you would do each of them. In explicating (making explicit) this practical knowledge, you will acquire further confidence in your ability to do them.

Let's end this chapter with a quiz:

Exercise 1.4: Recapping Chapter One

1. What is the definition of 'argument' that we are using in this book?

2. What is the 'frame test' for a declarative sentence?

3. Why is the sentence 'If she is a professional soprano she should be able to reach top A' not analysable as an argument?

4. One of the forces with which we can use a sentence is the assertoric force. Can you name two others?

5. How, in writing, do we usually show that we are mentioning a sentence rather than using it?

6. What is a truth value?

7. The parts of a simple sentence are all……………..?

8. The *weak* meaning of a sentence is given by its……..?

9. In acting we are guided by our beliefs but motivated by……?

10. The Principle of Charity is important because it reminds us that in the appearance of …………………..we have evidence for error.

Answers on page 353

Excellent! You have finished Chapter One. In Chapter Two we shall learn how to analyse arguments.

CHAPTER TWO

Analysing Arguments

This chapter corresponds to the second podcast in my series **'Critical Reasoning: A Romp Through the Nature of Arguments'**. The video podcast can be found at metafore.com/CR2video, the audio-only podcast at metafore.com/CR2audio, slides at metafore.com/ CR2slides and a transcript at mariannetalbot.co.uk/ transcripts/.

One of the most important things you'll learn in critical reasoning is how to analyse arguments. This is because an analysed argument is far easier to evaluate than an argument that is still in its everyday form.

In daily life when we use arguments, we suppress premises, we hedge our premises and conclusions with irrelevancies and we use inconsistent terminology. These confusions are made worse by the fact that we often put forward several arguments at once. So not only do we present our main argument, we simultaneously argue for our premises. Even worse, we rarely restrict ourselves to *making* arguments; we usually express our feelings about our arguments as we give them.

The result is a mishmash of words, most of which serve to *obscure* rather than clarify our argument. Yet in critical reasoning we get nowhere without clarity.

To analyse an argument is to set it out 'logic-book style' in such a way that it is clear:

- exactly what a person using the argument would be claiming;

- which reasons they would be offering to support their claim.

An analysed argument contains no ambiguities or irrelevancies, all its terminology is consistent and if any premise is suppressed it will be one that is such common knowledge its suppression is not problematic.

In learning how to set out an argument logic-book style you will learn how to identify conclusions and premises; how to eliminate irrelevancies, cross-references and inconsistent terminology; and when and how to make suppressed premises explicit.

First, though, we will have a look at ambiguity. We shall learn about the different types of ambiguity. We shall also learn how to disambiguate sentences with ambiguities of various types. We shall also consider why ambiguity of any type, is problematic for anyone who wants to analyse an argument.

By the end of this chapter you will be able to:

- recognise different types of ambiguity;

- detect and eliminate ambiguity;

- set out arguments 'logic-book style';

- recognise premise and conclusion 'indicators';

- identify conclusions by the role they play in an argument;

- recognise premises by the role they play in an argument;

- recognise and remove irrelevancies;

- recognise when a suppressed premise should be made explicit;

- analyse simple arguments and set them out logic-book style.

This is a lot of work to be done before we finish this chapter, so here we go....

Ambiguity

Here is the definition of 'ambiguous':

Def: **a word or phrase is** *ambiguous* **if it has more than one meaning.**

If a sentence contains an ambiguous word or phrase this means that the sentence will admit of different interpretations. It will have at least two interpretations, but as words and phrases can be *multiply ambiguous* it might have even more.

There are different types of ambiguity. In the next exercise you will learn something about them.

Here are six ambiguous sentences:

1. Every good girl loves a sailor.

2. She thought it was rum.

3. The black taxi drivers are on strike.

4. Jane invited Sara for tea but she said she had to go out for lunch.

5. I went to the bank.

6. Jaz doesn't want Jane at the party because she doesn't like her.

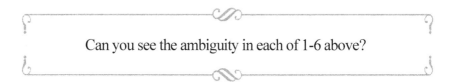

Can you see the ambiguity in each of 1-6 above?

Structural Ambiguity

Sentences 1 and 3 are both *structural* ambiguities. It is in the way the words in these sentences are combined that the ambiguities lie.

> **Def:** a *structural ambiguity* is an ambiguity that occurs when the words of a sentence can be grouped together differently.

So sentence 1 (Every good girl loves a sailor) has two interpretations as follows:

1a. There is a sailor such that every girl loves him.

1b. Every girl is such that there is a sailor she loves.

This ambiguity is clearly important. Is there just one lucky sailor who is loved by every girl? Or is it rather that every girl loves a different sailor?

Sentence 3 (The black taxi drivers are on strike) can be interpreted in either of these ways:

3a. The drivers of the black taxis are on strike.

3b. Those taxi drivers who are black are on strike.

Again this ambiguity might matter. If you were a union official you wouldn't want your press release to give journalists the wrong end of the stick.

We disambiguate a structural ambiguity by rewriting the sentence in each (or all) of the ways it could be understood and hoping that we can tell, from the context, which is the right interpretation.

Lexical Ambiguity

Sentences 2 and 5 on the other hand involve a *lexical ambiguity*. Here is the definition you need:

> **Def:** A *lexical ambiguity* **occurs when one word in a sentence can be understood in different ways.**

Sentence 2 (She thought it was rum) for example, can be understood as either:

2a. She thought it was strange.

2b. She thought it was rum (rather than vodka).

Sentence 5 (I went to the bank) on the other hand can be understood as either:

5a. I went to the river bank.

5b. I went to the financial institution.

We disambiguate lexical ambiguities by making it clear which interpretation we mean. If we have to use both words in an argument we would distinguish them by subscripts ($bank_1$, $bank_2$) Again the context would probably make it clear which meaning was intended. We might, though, have to ask the speaker what she meant.

Ambiguity of Cross Reference

Sentences 4 and 6 are ambiguities of cross reference. In both these sentences some word refers back to something mentioned earlier in the sentence, but it is unclear exactly what it is that is being referred to again.

Def: an *ambiguity of cross reference* occurs when it is unclear to which word a later word refers back.

Sentence 4 (Jane invited Sara for tea but she said she had to go out for lunch) is multiply ambiguous. It could be understood as:

4a. Jane invited Sara for tea but Jane said she (Jane) had to go out for lunch.

4b Jane invited Sara for tea but Jane said she (Sara) had to go out for lunch.

4c. Jane invited Sara for tea but Sara said she (Sara) had to go out for lunch.

4d. Jane invited Sara for tea but Sara said she (Jane) had to go out for lunch.

Sentence 6. on the other hand could be either:

6a. Jaz doesn't want Jane at the party because Jane doesn't like Jaz.

6b. Jaz doesn't want Jane at the party because Jaz doesn't like Jane.

We disambiguate ambiguities of cross reference by making it clear which reference it is that we are picking up again.

Spoken Ambiguity

Ambiguities can also arise when we speak. This can happen when two different words sound alike. For example if you heard either of the following sentences you might not know which sentence you were hearing:

- A pitcher of water

- A picture of water

You might be able to tell from the context whether we were talking about works of art or containers of liquid, or again you would have to ask.

Sometimes it is by our emphasis that we disambiguate a sentence. Try emphasising different words of the following question:

Do *swallows* fly south for winter? Do swallows *fly* south for winter? Do swallows fly *south* for winter? Do swallows fly south for *winter*?

You should have found that with each difference in emphasis you get a question demanding a different answer.

In the podcast I also identified ambiguities of *pragmatics* (slide 8 of podcast 2). This is the ambiguity that arises when we use a word or phrase to do different things. I covered this, albeit not under this name, when I talked of *force* in chapter one.

Context

You will have noticed that an ambiguous sentence is usually disambiguated by the context in which it appears. But it might already have started to worry you (well done if it has!) that it is only *assertions* that are used in a context. Declarative sentences are only *mentioned* not used, so they don't have a context in the same way.

Sentences 1-6 discussed above were all declarative sentences, so they weren't uttered in a context of use. This was why they were such good examples; you could see immediately that they were ambiguous. If they were being used in a context that disambiguated them you might have failed to realise that they were ambiguous.

Here is an illustration (adapted from Daniel Kahneman's book 'Thinking Fast and Slow') of how context can disambiguate a figure without our noticing:

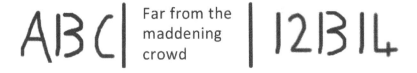

Professor Kahneman suggests that you might have read the middle figure as a 'B' on the left hand side, but as a '13' on the right hand side. Yet the two figures, he points out, are identical. If you saw the former as a 'B' this will be because you read it in the context of other letters. If you read the latter as a '13' this will be because you read it in the context of other numbers.

Sometimes we disambiguate things so readily in context that we don't even know we are doing it.

50

> *Kahneman's book is a fascinating discussion of two different ways of thinking. I recommend it to you. It can be bought on Amazon here:metafore.com/cr/dk. If you'd like to read more about ambiguity you might try: metafore.com/cr/stana*

In studying critical reasoning it is important to avoid using ambiguous sentences. Clarity really is of the essence in critical reasoning, and anything that could lead to confusion should be avoided.

The next set of exercises will enable you to test your ability to recognise and eliminate ambiguity.

Exercise 2.1: Disambiguate the following sentences by providing two or more sentences each of which is a different interpretation of the sentence. Then identify the type of ambiguity involved in each sentence.

1. Only rich men can stay here

2. The Headteacher can't bear children

3. Some women only go to the theatre with men who treat them politely

4. The student read the essay to the tutor and he was bored by it

5. Irritating children should be banned

6. James is the only man who does not admire his mother

7. He saw her duck

Answers on page 355

Analysing Arguments

To analyse an argument is to set it out logic-book style. You may remember this from chapter one where we analysed a complex sentence as an argument as follows:

Premise one: The mail is always late when it rains

Premise two: It is raining

Conclusion: The mail will be late.

You can see that when an argument is set out like this we know exactly which sentence is playing the role of the conclusion of the argument (i.e. which sentence is being asserted on the basis of the others). We also know exactly which sentence(s) are playing the role of the reasons for believing the conclusion; the premises.

As we saw in the introduction, arguments in every day life are not usually anything like this. When you are in the café with your friend you are more likely to hear an argument like this:

"If the German Government lasts the year then the moon is made of green cheese. Even though there is no opposition, the economy is going to the dogs and Herr Kohl is about to be humiliated by his EC partners. Certainly, if the economy flourishes, his Government will survive. But grass roots support will inevitably fade if Herr Kohl is humiliated, and unless he gets that support, his Government will only last in a flourishing economy."[2]

There is (I promise you) an argument hidden in amongst all the verbiage here. Our challenge in the rest of this chapter is to find it.

---

[2] Example adapted from the Philosophy Prelims Paper, 1993, University of Oxford.

Having found it we will set it out logic-book style. I will refer to this argument as 'the target argument'. As we analyse it you will see that at each stage the structure of the target argument becomes clearer. In later chapters we shall formalise and evaluate this argument.

So what do we need to do to set out this argument (and any other argument) logic-book style? Well, there are 6 steps we must take. We must:

1. identify the conclusion of the argument;

2. identify the premises of the argument;

3. remove cross references (if there are any);

4. eliminate any irrelevancies (if there are any);

5. remove inconsistent terminology (if there is any);

6. explicate malign suppressed premises (if there are any).

In the rest of this chapter we shall do just this with this argument. As we do so we will learn the techniques that will enable us to analyse any argument.

Step One: Identifying Conclusions

You will remember from chapter one the definition of the *conclusion* of an argument. The conclusion is the sentence that would be being asserted by one who was using the argument. It is the sentence which is being argued *for.*

You should be aware that you cannot tell which sentence is the conclusion by its position in the argument. Conclusions can be at the beginning of the argument, they can be in the middle or they can be at the end of the argument. It is only when set out logic-book style that they are *always* at the end of the argument. If you are watching the podcasts slides 16 and 17 (of podcast two) have the following examples of arguments where the conclusions are not at the end of the argument:

Marianne is wearing jeans because it is Friday and Marianne always wears jeans on Friday

It is Friday so Marianne is wearing jeans because Marianne always wears jeans on Friday

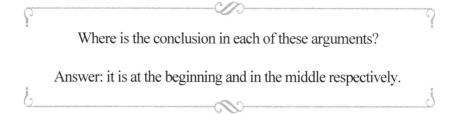

Where is the conclusion in each of these arguments?

Answer: it is at the beginning and in the middle respectively.

The other thing you should note is that a sentence that is the conclusion of one argument might be a premise in another argument. There is *no* sentence that is, by its very nature, a conclusion; every sentence can be asserted, every sentence is such that we can offer reasons for believing that it is true, and every sentence can be a reason for believing the truth of another sentence.

You should always start analysing an argument by looking for the conclusion of the argument. Everything else you do in analysing the argument follows from the conclusion. Once you have the conclusion, for example, you will find it much easier to find the premises and to determine which words in the argument, as given, are irrelevant to the argument being made.

Luckily, conclusions are often indicated by words like 'so' 'hence' or 'therefore'. Sadly conclusions are not always indicated in this way.

The only foolproof way of finding the conclusion of an argument is by the role played by the sentence in the argument. You will be looking, of course, for the sentence that is being asserted on the basis of the other sentences.

If you are having trouble it might help to read out the argument as if you were the person using it. Read it out *with feeling* as if you really were using it. That will often help you to find what it is you would be arguing for if you were using the argument in question.

In the target argument which sentence is playing the role of the conclusion?

My answer follows shortly.

"If the German Government lasts the year then the moon is made of green cheese. Even though there is no opposition, the economy is going to the dogs and Herr Kohl is about to be humiliated by his EC partners. Certainly, if the economy flourishes, his Government will survive. But grass roots support will inevitably fade if Herr Kohl is humiliated, and unless he gets that support, his Government will only last in a flourishing economy."

In podcast two (slide 23) I summarise the five things you need to know to identify the conclusion of an argument.

Exercise 2.2: Identifying Conclusions.

Identify the conclusion in each of the following arguments (remember you are not being asked to evaluate the arguments we are looking at yet):

1. During the game he committed a serious foul, so he deserved to be sent off.

2. Women's brains are on average smaller than men's brains, therefore women are less intelligent than men.

3. The Butler couldn't have done it. After all he was in the pantry, and the Count was in his study.

4. The green movement is wrong to think we should recycle paper because paper comes from trees which are renewable. Recycling paper has been abandoned in many American cities because it is too expensive.

Answers on page 357

Did you succeed, by the way, in identifying the conclusion of our target argument the one about Herr Kohl and his Government?

In order to get this you would have had to understand the colloquialism with which the argument starts: the claim that 'if the German Government lasts the year then the moon is made of green cheese.' Any English speaker hearing this sentence would know immediately that the declarative sentence that would capture the belief being expressed by one uttering this sentence would be 'the German Government won't last the year'. This is the conclusion of this argument:

Conclusion: The German Government won't last the year.

This conclusion wasn't indicated by any 'conclusion indicator'. It wasn't to be found at the end of the argument either. Both these things should remind you that the only foolproof way to identify a conclusion is by the role it is playing in the argument i.e. by virtue of the fact that it is the claim being asserted, the one for which reasons are being offered.

Having identified our conclusion, we can now move onto our next step:

Step Two: Identifying Premises

Our next task is to identify the premises of our argument. Once you have identified the conclusions, identifying the premises is usually fairly easy. They will usually be the sentences left after the conclusion has been taken out of the argument. (It is true that sometimes one or more of the sentences left are irrelevant to the argument, but we can worry about that later when we deal with 'irrelevancies'.)

Premises are often indicated by 'premise indicators', words and phrases like 'because', 'for the reason that' and 'after all'. Again, though, you cannot guarantee that there will be premise indicators. Also, as with conclusions, you cannot identify premises by their position in the argument; they can be at the beginning of the argument, at its end, or they can sandwich the conclusion between them by being at the beginning *and* the end.

There is no rule about the number of premises an argument has, except that it must have at least one. An argument might have one premise, or it might have 10. It could even have 20 (though I promise I shan't present you with any such arguments in this book).

Again, therefore, the only foolproof way to identify the premises of an argument is by the role they play in the argument. The premises of the argument *always* play the role of supporting the conclusion; they will always be *reasons* for believing the conclusion.

One complication that often arises when trying to identify the premises of an argument is what you should do when one of the sentences that remains after the conclusion has been removed is a conjunction. You will note, when you attempt to identify the premises of the target argument that this is just such an argument.

Here is the definition of 'conjunction':

> **Def:** a *conjunction* is a complex sentence formed by means of two simple sentences and the logical word 'and'.

Be careful about the word 'and' because it can conjoin two predicates (words for properties), as in 'the cat was black and white'. This *doesn't* mean 'the cat was black *and* the cat was white'. We don't have two simple sentences here conjoined by an 'and'. Here the 'and' conjoins the predicates 'black' and 'white'.

The complication I am talking about here only arises when the 'and' conjoins *sentences.* Here is a sentence in which this is the case:

(1) The journey was long and tiring.

A moment's thought will tell you that you can analyse this sentence as 'the journey was long *and* the journey was tiring'. The 'and' here, despite appearances, is not conjoining two predicates, it is conjoining two simple sentences.

Exercise 2.3: 'And' Conjoining Predicates or Sentences?

Please say whether the following sentences can be analysed as a conjunction of two sentences:

1. They visited Cairo and Luxor.

2. The dress was blue and green.

3. He and his twin were both clever.

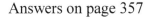

Answers on page 357

If you come across a conjunction when you are analysing an argument you might wonder whether to leave the conjunction as just *one* premise (a complex sentence), or to treat each conjoined sentence as a premise in its own right (two simple sentences).

The answer is that you should split the conjunction if both conjuncts are needed for the conclusion of the argument to follow.

At the moment, though, we are not looking at what it is for a conclusion to follow from a set of premises, so for now you should always split conjunctions, treating each conjunct as a premise in its own right. You should only do this, of course, if the 'and' really is conjoining two independent sentences, rather than two predicates.

Now you might like to have a go at identifying the premises of the target argument.

**In the target argument which sentences are playing
the role of the premises?**

My answer is below.

"Even though there is no opposition, the economy is going to
the dogs and Herr Kohl is about to be humiliated by his EC
partners. Certainly, if the economy flourishes, his Government
will survive. But grass roots support will inevitably fade if Herr
Kohl is humiliated, and unless he gets that support, his
Government will only last in a flourishing economy."

Before I give you the answer to which sentences are the premises
of the target argument you might like to do the exercise on the
following page:

Exercise 2.4: Identifying Premises

In the exercise above you identified the conclusion of the
following arguments.
You should now identify the premise(s).
(Remember you are still not being asked to evaluate the
arguments):

1. During the game he committed a serious foul, so he
    deserved to be sent off.

2. Women's brains are on average smaller than men's,
    therefore women are less intelligent than men.

3. The Butler couldn't have done it. After all he was in the
    pantry, and the Count was in his study.

4. The green movement is wrong to think we should recycle
    paper because paper comes from trees which are
    renewable. Recycling paper has been abandoned in many
    American cities because it is too expensive.

Answers on page 358

Did you succeed in identifying the premises of the target argument. Here are the premises as I understand them:

Premise one: Even though there is no opposition, the economy is going to the dogs

Premise two: Herr Kohl is about to be humiliated by his EC partners

Premise three: Certainly, if the economy flourishes, his Government will survive

Premise four: But grass roots support will inevitably fade if Herr Kohl is humiliated

Premise five: Unless he gets that support, his Government will only last in a flourishing economy

Did you get the premises? You will notice that I have simply split up all the sentences left in the argument after the conclusion was removed, and that the only words I have left out are the 'and's that conjoined premises one and two, and premises four and five. I can leave out these 'and's because they are implied by the fact that each of the conjoined sentences appears as a separate premise in the argument.

On slide 46 of podcast two I list the seven things you need to know to identify the premises of an argument.

We can now set out logic-book style the premises and conclusion of our target argument. All we have to do is add the conclusion we identified above to the end of our list of premises, labelling it 'conclusion'.

Here is the argument with premises *and* conclusion:

Premise one: Even though there is no opposition, the economy is going to the dogs

Premise two: Herr Kohl is about to be humiliated by his EC partners

Premise three: Certainly, if the economy flourishes, his Government will survive

Premise four: But grass roots support will inevitably fade if Herr Kohl is humiliated

Premise Five: Unless he gets that support, his Government will only last in a flourishing economy

Conclusion: The German Government won't last the year.

But the argument is not yet fully analysed. We can't call an argument fully analysed until we have removed cross references, irrelevancies and inconsistent terms, and until we have checked the argument for suppressed premises. We'll learn how to do these things next, starting with the cross references.

Step Three: Remove Cross References

We came across the notion of a cross reference when we talked about ambiguity. We use a cross reference whenever we use a word or phrase as a shorthand way of referring back to someone (or something) already introduced.

In any informal argument like our target argument, the person using the argument will almost always use these shorthand references because it is tedious, both for the speaker and the audience, to spell everything out rather than to use a pronoun such as 'you' 'he', or 'I' or a demonstrative such as 'this' and 'that'.

When we are analysing arguments, though, we want to put ourselves as far as we can into a situation in which the conclusion and each of the premises is a complete sentence with meaning in its own right. This demands that we remove all the cross references that ensure that the words of one sentence have meaning only by reference to the words of *another sentence* in the argument.

Sometimes the cross reference appears in one of the simple sentences of which a complex sentence is constituted. Here the cross-reference occurs *within* a sentence rather than *across* sentences. We should remove this one too. Doing so will make the sentence read rather clumsily, but getting into the habit of removing *all* cross references will make life easier for us when it comes to formalising the argument. This is a *long* way ahead yet, but we may as well get ourselves into pole position!

The following sentence is a complex sentence constituted of two simple sentences and the logical words 'if and only if':

(1) Sam's party will finish at midnight if and only if his parents get home by then.

The two simple sentences that constitute this complex sentence are:

(a) Sam's party will finish at midnight.

(b) His parents get home at that time.

If we split the complex sentence into its constituent sentences, however, we might lose the fact that the 'parents' we are talking about are *Sam's* parents, or that '*that time*' is midnight. The argument might, for example, also refer to someone else's parents, and/or to another time. To make sure we do not lose sight of the fact these are Sam's parents, and that the time is midnight, we remove the cross references as follows:

(2) Sam's party will finish at midnight if and only if Sam's parents get home by midnight.

I hope you'll agree that (2) has the same meaning as (1) even if (2) is a bit clunkier.

The need to remove cross-references does not mean that we need to remove every instance of a pronoun. In argument 1 of the exercises we have been doing above, for example, we were introduced to the person under discussion only as 'he'.

Argument 1.   During the game he committed a serious foul, so he deserved to be sent off.

We could introduce a name for this player ('During the game Fred committed a serious foul, so Fred deserved to be sent off') but it is simpler just to stick to talking of him as 'he' unless we think that, in the context of the argument we are analysing, this might confuse us.

Exercise 2.5: Eliminating Cross References

Can you eliminate the cross references from our target
argument?

NOTE: There might not be a cross-reference in which case you
shouldn't add anything.

Premise one: Even though there is no opposition, the
economy is going to the dogs

Premise two: Herr Kohl is about to be humiliated by his EC
partners

Premise three: Certainly, if the economy flourishes, his
Government will survive

Premise four: But grass roots support will inevitably fade if
Herr Kohl is humiliated

Premise five: Unless he gets that support, his Government will
only last in a flourishing economy

Conclusion: The German Government won't last the year.

Answers on page 359

In my experience when people first start analysing arguments they
can tie themselves in knots by 'over-thinking'. It might occur to
you, for example, that 'the economy' in premise one must mean
the *German* economy, and this might tempt you to add the words
'of the German Government' to premise one.

But you were right in the first place: it is *obvious* that the economy in question is the German economy. In fact we stipulated in chapter one that within the context of one argument we shall always assume that we are talking about the same subject matter. The fact that it is obvious we are talking about the German economy, therefore, means that we needn't make it explicit.

The only exception to this would be if the argument talked about two economies, and we needed to make it clear that this particular one is the German economy. That isn't the case with this argument.

You might immediately object that it is obvious, too, that 'the parents' of sentence (1) above are Sam's parents. This is true, so long as we do not split up the sentence into its constituent parts and treat each as an independent sentence. But this is exactly what we are going to do when we start to formalise arguments, so please bear with me: remove cross references that actually appear within an argument but do not start adding words to premises to make even more obvious something that is already obvious!

Step Four: eliminating irrelevancies

It is often the elimination of irrelevancies that starts to make a huge difference to an argument under analysis. If there are a lot of irrelevancies in the original argument, the removal of them will reveal the structure of the argument much more clearly. You will discover that this is not particularly the case with the target argument.

Bear in mind, as you look for irrelevancies, that our aim is to reveal the conclusion of the argument, and the reasons being offered for it, as clearly as possible.

So we need to look for words and phrases that merely 'pad out' the argument, adding nothing to the reasons being given for the conclusion of the argument, or indeed to the conclusion itself.

You will often find words that are used simply to add emphasis. For example 'I know that the cat is on the mat' sometimes means nothing more than that the cat is on the mat. This is the case, for example, in the following argument:

Argument 2.1:

Premise one: If the cat is on the mat then the dog isn't around

Premise two: I know that the cat is on the mat

Conclusion: The dog isn't around.

The words 'I know that' play no role in this argument. The *knowledge* that the cat is on the mat is irrelevant to the argument. All that is needed for the argument is that the cat *is* on the mat.

Be careful about this, though, because sometimes the argument *will* be about the speaker's knowledge that the cat is on the mat, rather than just that the cat is on the mat. In the following case, for example, the words 'I know that' are *not* irrelevant.

Argument 2.2:

Premise one: To have knowledge is to have a justified, true belief

Premise two: I know that the cat is on the mat

Conclusion: I have a justified true belief that the cat is on the mat.

I hope you can see that in this case the words 'I know that' are far from irrelevant?

It is not always easy to tell the difference between the first case (where 'I know that' *isn't* relevant) and the second case (where 'I know that' *is* relevant). Remember though that your aim is to reveal, as clearly as possible, the conclusion of the argument and the reasons being given for that conclusion. Anything that contributes neither to the conclusion, nor to the reasons being offered for it, can be left out.

Sometimes it might take some thought to realise that words are not adding anything to the meaning (except perhaps emphasis). For example, can you see that in the sentence 'Even if the dog is home the cat is on the mat' the words 'even if the dog is home' are irrelevant. This is because 'even if P, Q' means that Q is true *whether or not P is true*. 'Even if P, Q' amounts to nothing more than 'Q'.

Sometimes whole sentences are irrelevant. For example if you come across the following in an argument:

Premise one: If you thought that you're an idiot, but you are not an idiot.

You can probably see that it cancels itself out. It says '*if* something is true...', and then adds that this something *isn't* true. In such a case we can safely eliminate the whole sentence as irrelevant.

Please eliminate any irrelevancies you can find in the target argument:

Premise one: Even though there is no opposition, the economy is going to the dogs

Premise two: Herr Kohl is about to be humiliated by his EC partners

Premise three: Certainly if the economy flourishes the German Government will survive.

Premise four: But grass roots support will inevitably fade if Herr Kohl is humiliated

Premise five: Unless Herr Kohl gets grass roots support, the German Government will only last in a flourishing economy

Conclusion: The German Government won't last the year.

Some arguments (but not the target argument) are such that we also need to look for and eliminate 'sub-arguments'. This too might involve eliminating whole sentences.

These sub-arguments occur when, in an argument, a person offers reasons, not just for believing the conclusion, but also for believing one or more of the premises. This is the case, for example, in this argument:

Premise one: If the dog is at home the cat won't be on the mat

Premise two: The cat is on the mat

Premise three: I know the cat is on the mat because I just saw her there

Conclusion: The dog is not home.

Can you see that the sentence labelled 'premise three' here is not a reason for believing the conclusion? It is a reason for believing premise two. As such it is not required for the argument we are concerned with, and can be eliminated. (We might need to consider it again when we come to ask whether the premises are true, but we are not evaluating arguments just yet).

Exercise 2.6: Eliminating Irrelevancies

Please set out the following argument logic-book style, eliminating irrelevancies as you go (remember you are not evaluating the argument yet):

The snowdrops don't come out until spring, though they are often the first flowers to appear. The garden is beautiful at the moment, there are crocuses, snowdrops, the daffodils are beginning to bud and the cat is being driven mad by the catkins dancing in the breeze. Spring has sprung!

Answers on page 360

How did you do at eliminating the irrelevancies from the target argument? I have put in **bold** all the words and phrases that I would eliminate:

Premise one: Even though there is no opposition, the economy is going to the dogs

Premise two: Herr Kohl is about to be humiliated **by his EC** partners

Premise three: If the economy flourishes the German Government will survive

Premise four: Grass roots support will inevitably fade if Herr Kohl is humiliated

Premise five: Unless Herr Kohl gets grass roots support, the German Government will only last in a flourishing economy

Conclusion: The German Government won't last the year.

You might be surprised that I have removed the whole of premise three. I have done this because this premises says that if the economy flourishes then the German Government will survive. But premise one has already told us that the economy is not flourishing so the state of affairs that would obtain were the economy to flourish is irrelevant.

You might also question my removal of the cause of Herr Kohl's humiliation ('by his EC partners'). I have done so because it plays no role in the argument (although it is certainly interesting to anyone who is interested in the content of the argument).

Please don't worry if you didn't get this. Don't even worry if you still don't get it now I have explained it. The worse that can happen is that you will not have removed an irrelevancy. This will probably make the argument harder to evaluate, but it is unlikely to make it impossible.

Once I remove the irrelevant words and phrases from the argument this is the result:

Premise one: The economy is going to the dogs

Premise two: Herr Kohl is about to be humiliated

Premise three: Grass roots support will inevitably fade if Herr Kohl is humiliated

Premise four: Unless Herr Kohl gets grass roots support, the German Government will only last in a flourishing economy

Conclusion: The German Government won't last the year.

Step Five: Removing Inconsistent Terminology

Our penultimate task is to remove inconsistent terminology. The words 'consistent' and 'inconsistent' are ambiguous. We will discover later in this book they can be used to say, respectively, of a set of sentences that they can all be true together (i.e. that there is a possible situation in which all are true), or that they *cannot* all be true together (i.e. that there isn't a possible situation in which all are true together).

But this is not how we are using the words here. In analysing an argument we want to try to eliminate as many distractions as we can. When two different words or phrases are used to mean the same thing this is a distraction. We talk about such terminology as 'inconsistent'. When we have made an argument such that the same words or phrases are used to mean the same thing throughout the argument, we will talk of its terminology as *consistent.*

For example if we find, in one premise of any argument, the words 'the mailman', and in another premise the words 'the postman', nothing is going to be lost if we choose just one of these phrases to use in both premises. In fact we will gain because we will not be distracted by having to make use of two different words for the same thing.

Let's now remove the inconsistent terminology from our target argument.

Exercise 2.7: Eliminating Inconsistent Terminology.

Please eliminate the inconsistent terminology from our target argument:

Premise one: The economy is going to the dogs

Premise two: Herr Kohl is about to be humiliated

Premise three: Grass roots support will inevitably fade if Herr Kohl is humiliated

Premise four: Unless Herr Kohl gets grass roots support, the German Government will only last in a flourishing economy

Conclusion: The German Government won't last the year.

Answers on page 361

Our target argument is starting to look truly skeletal now. Good! That is how we hope that an analysed argument will look. You can probably already see that the argument we're dealing with now is much easier to evaluate than the argument with which we started. In fact you might even be able to say whether you think the conclusion follows from the premises. I doubt you were able to do that when you first came across the argument.

Step Six: Explicating Suppressed Premises

When, in chapter one, we discussed beliefs and reasons you will probably have realised that you have literally thousands of beliefs of which you are unaware. The belief 'zebras don't carry handbags' was the example I used there of a belief of yours of which you were (probably) unaware.

When we discussed the Principle of Charity, again in chapter one, you were told that in interpreting another person you should always try for the interpretation on which their beliefs were (largely) true *by your lights*. In other words, you should treat as suspicious any interpretation on which your companion does not share your beliefs.

These two things are linked in the recognition that we can nearly always assume that another person will share many of our beliefs, certainly about the immediate environment.

Human beings may be very different from each other, but we share our world. It is likely, furthermore, that we share, with most of those around us, a language and a culture. It is hugely likely that all human beings share their belief-forming apparatus; it has after all evolved and is likely, therefore, to be species-specific. It would be astonishing, therefore, if we *didn't* share many beliefs.

This saves us a huge amount of time and energy because we can *assume* that anyone we are talking to will believe many of the things we believe. This saves us from having to spell out these beliefs.

In arguing for something (and with someone), in particular, to the extent we can be sure that a belief is shared, we can leave that belief implicit. The more likely it is that a belief is shared the less need there is to make that belief explicit in an argument.

In everyday life, therefore, nearly every argument is an *enthymeme*, an argument with a suppressed premise.

Def: **an *enthymeme* is an argument with a suppressed premise.**

In analysing an argument however, you need only make these suppressed premises explicit if they are controversial. If they are controversial, after all, then we do *not* know that the person with whom we are arguing will share our belief.

Exercise 2.8: Identifying Suppressed Premises

You have already identified the premises and the conclusions of the following arguments.

Will you now identify any premises that have been left implicit and say whether you think they are controversial:

1. During the game he committed a serious foul, so he deserved to be sent off.

2. Women's brains are on average smaller than men's, therefore women are less intelligent than men.

3. The butler couldn't have done it. After all he was in the pantry, and the count was in his study.

4. The green movement is wrong to think we should recycle paper because paper comes from trees which are renewable. Recycling paper has been abandoned in many American cities because it is too expensive.

Answers on page 362

It can, of course, be difficult to decide when a premise is controversial. This is partly because, given that so many beliefs are shared, our default position is one on which we assume a belief is shared until we learn otherwise. You may have experienced a strange sense of dislocation when, in conversation, with another person, you realise they *don't* share a belief the truth of which you had always taken for granted.

If you are in doubt, therefore, about whether a premise should be made explicit or not, you should play safe and make it explicit. But do not go mad. We do not want arguments with 20 premises, most of which should have been left implicit!

Are there any suppressed premises in our target argument?

You'll find my answer below.

Premise one: The economy is not flourishing

Premise two: Herr Kohl is humiliated

Premise three: Herr Kohl will not get grass roots support if Herr Kohl is humiliated

Premise four: Unless Herr Kohl gets grass roots support, the German Government will only last in a flourishing economy

Conclusion: The German Government won't last the year.

Deciding whether a suppressed premise is benign and such therefore that it needn't be made explicit, or controversial and such therefore that it *must* be made explicit, is a matter of judgement.

As you gain in experience the judgement will become easier.

Did you decide there is no controversial suppressed premise in our target argument I hope so, because if this is what you decided you would be right! Well done.

Analysing Simple Arguments

You have now learned all the techniques you need to analyse arguments. All you need now is practice. Our next exercise, the last one in this chapter, gives you some simple arguments to practise on.

If you are having difficulty you should bear in mind that you are almost certainly trying to be too clever. You may be seeing irrelevancies that are not – er – relevant (i.e. that do not matter to the argument). You may be trying to make consistent terms that are consistent enough. You may be trying to explicate premises that are not controversial. Whilst it cannot be said that analysing an argument is *simple*, it is not as difficult as beginners often make it.

If you are having difficulties, therefore, go back over the relevant part of the chapter and try to see *why* you are doing what you are doing. Having discovered the purpose of the activity, do not try to do more than is required to attain the purpose.

Exercise 2.9: Analysing Simple Arguments

Please set out the following arguments logic-book style, removing irrelevancies, cross references and inconsistent terms and adding any controversial suppressed premises:

1. The dog only ever barks when it sees a stranger, but then boy! Does it bark! In fact it is making a terrible noise right now, so unless it has gone mad it must be able to see someone it doesn't know coming up the drive.

2. Mungo is completely potty about the Big Bang Theory but Joanna likes to watch the News. As both programmes are on at 6pm, they will have to buy another television (which is probably too expensive for them) or agree to compromise.

3. As I was driving home the car started to make a strange noise. It was really quite frightening. I can see that I am going to have to economise.

Answers on page 363

If your version is not quite the same as mine, it is fine as long as the meanings are preserved.

Did you get these right? Now let's check that we can do everything we are supposed to be able to do:

- recognise different types of ambiguity;

- detect and eliminate ambiguity;

- set out arguments 'logic-book style';

- recognise premise and conclusion 'indicators';

- identify conclusions by the role they play in an argument;

- recognise premises by the role they play in an argument;

- recognise and remove irrelevancies;

- recognise when a suppressed premise should be made explicit;

- analyse simple arguments and set them out logic book style.

Don't forget you may not feel confident about all these things – that comes with practice – but unless you'd like to go back to check the things you're unsure about, let's move on to chapter three!

CHAPTER THREE

Arguments of Two Types

This chapter corresponds to the third podcast in my series:
Critical Reasoning: A Romp Through The Foothills of Logic.
The video podcast can be found at metafore.com/CR3video, the
audio-only podcast at metafore.com/CR3audio, slides at
metafore.com/CR3slides and a transcript at http://
mariannetalbot.co.uk/transcripts/.

Warning: Podcast Complication

In the podcast I was trying, for some reason, to avoid the term
'validity'. I referred instead to 'truth-preservingness'. I can't
remember why I did this. It complicates everything. Please forget
the notion of truth-preservingness in favour of the notion of
validity that you'll be taught below.

You now know what arguments are, and you are able to analyse
them (after a bit more practice, perhaps). You've come a long way.

In this chapter we are going to learn that all arguments fall into one of two categories. They will either be deductive or they will be inductive. Some have suggested that *abductive arguments* are a third category. I believe these are inductive arguments and shall argue for this claim. You might disagree with me.

In this chapter you will also learn that good deductive arguments are called 'valid', bad ones 'invalid', and that inductive arguments are neither valid nor invalid.

This vocabulary is sometimes used differently. Some authors, for example, talk about *inductive* validity. In this book we shall be sticking to the definitions given here. They are those used by most philosophers.

When you have carefully read this chapter you should be able to:

- distinguish between arguments that are good and arguments that are sound;

- say what is involved in a conclusion following from a set of premises;

- describe two types of 'following from': deductive and inductive;

- explain the difference between logical and empirical possibility;

- explain why deduction is an either/or matter, whilst induction isn't;

- explain what is meant by 'deduction gives us certainty, induction only probability';

- explain why good deductive arguments are conclusive, inductive argument not;

- explain the notions of 'a priori' and 'a posteriori';

- explain what it is to evaluate arguments a priori and a posteriori.

As usual we will pause at the end of the chapter for you to check you really can do these things.

Evaluating Arguments

Human beings argue in the hope of acquiring knowledge. Arguments help us do this only if they satisfy two conditions:

1. their premises are true;

2. their conclusions follow from the premises.

Some arguments satisfy both these conditions but *don't* enable us to acquire knowledge. We'll learn about these in chapter four. But satisfaction of both these conditions is *necessary,* even if it isn't sufficient, for us to acquire knowledge from an argument.

If an argument satisfies both conditions it is called 'sound'. If it satisfies condition 2, then regardless of the truth value of its premises, it is called 'good'. Here are the definitions:

> **Def:** **an argument is *sound* iff its premises are all true and its conclusion follows from its premises.**

> **Def:** **an argument is *good* iff its conclusion follows from its premises (irrespective of the truth of its premises).**

The word 'iff' is not a misspelling. It is a philosophers' abbreviation of the logical phrase 'if and only if'. You'll come across it often in this book.

You will see immediately that every sound argument is good, but not every good argument is sound. There are good arguments the premises of which are *not* true.

In daily life you probably *wouldn't* call an argument 'good' if its premises were false. In critical reasoning, however, our concern is with whether the conclusion of an argument follows from its premises. Because this is what matters we think of an argument as 'good' in virtue of its satisfying this condition, irrespective of the truth of its premises.

You might think 'but if the premises of an argument are false who cares whether or not its conclusion follows?'

Well, we often *disagree* about whether something is true or false, or sometimes we simply *don't know* whether something is true or false. In either case if an argument is good we can at least say that *if* the premises are true, then the conclusion follows. This gives us *conditional knowledge*. Conditional knowledge can be very useful.

Exercise 3.1: Using an intuitive notion of 'good' decide whether the following arguments are sound, good, neither or unknown?

If you don't know whether the premises are true just judge 'goodness'. We will be learning a more technical definition of 'good' shortly.

1. Grass is green, emeralds are green, therefore emeralds are the same colour as grass.

2. If it is summer the bees will be pollinating the flowers, the bees are pollinating the flowers, therefore it is summer.

3. The Prince of Wales will become King only when the Duke of Edinburgh dies. The Duke of Edinburgh may not die for a long time, therefore the Prince of Wales may not become King for a long time.

4. The Prince of Wales will become King only when the Duke of Edinburgh dies. The Prince of Wales may not become King for a long time, therefore the Duke of Edinburgh may not die for a long time.

Answers on page 364

We will be concerned only with *good* arguments. We will not worry about whether the premises of an argument are true. Our sole concern will be whether its conclusion *follows from* its premises.

The Relation of 'Following From'

Logic, because it talks about 'good' and 'bad' arguments, is a *normative* discipline. It appeals to *standards*, rejecting some arguments and accepting others. The ability to evaluate arguments is crucial.

'Following from' is an important relationship in evaluating arguments. An argument can be good if and *only* if its conclusion follows from its premises, i.e.:

1. if an argument is good its conclusion follows from its premises (this is a *sufficient* condition for the argument's being good);

2. an argument is good *only if* its conclusion follows from its premises (this is a *necessary* condition for the argument's being good).

The conclusion of an argument follows from its premises when and only when believing the premises of the argument rationally obliges us, to some degree, to believe the conclusion.

Here are two arguments – have a look at them to see what I mean by being 'rationally obliged' (to some degree) to believe a conclusion:

Argument 3.1:

Premise one: If it is spring the snowdrops will be out

Premise two: It is spring

Conclusion: The snowdrops will be out.

Argument 3.2:

Premise one: Everyone with Huntington's Disease ever genetically tested has had the HD gene on chromosome 4

Premise two: Freya has HD and is about to be genetically tested

Conclusion: Freya will be found to have the HD gene on chromosome four.

Anyone believing both the premises in either argument has good reason for believing the conclusion.

If you believe the premises of argument 3.1, in fact, you are rationally *bound* to believe the conclusion. To fail to believe the conclusion, despite believing the premises, is a failure of reason.

Someone who believes the premises of argument 3.2 isn't rationally *bound* to believe the conclusion. They might have reason to believe that there is a genetic variant of HD, and that Freya has the variant kind. In the absence of such defeating reasons, though, to believe the premises is to have reason to believe the conclusion.

To see that anyone accepting both the premises of these arguments is rationally bound, to some degree, to accept the conclusions is to see that the conclusions *follow from* the premises.

We noted in chapter one that the study of critical reasoning is the study of beliefs and the rational relations between them. It is, in particular, the study of the rational relation of 'following from'.

Two Types of Following From

Our primary concern in this chapter is not to evaluate arguments. It is to see that arguments are always either *deductive* or *inductive*. By the end of this chapter you will be able (perhaps with a bit of practice) to say, of any argument you come across, whether it is deductive or inductive.

The conclusion of argument 3.1 follows *deductively* from its premises. The conclusion of argument 3.2 follows *inductively* from its premises.

You may have heard of arguments from authority, arguments from analogy, syllogisms, modus ponens and other argument-types. Deduction and induction are the two 'highest' categories. Every argument falls into one or other of these types, before it falls into any of the sub-categories mentioned.

The Differences Between Deduction and Induction

Three characteristics distinguish deductive arguments from inductive:

Deductive arguments are:	Inductive arguments are:
Either good or bad	Good or bad to some degree
Conclusive, so they give certainty	Inconclusive, so they give only probability
Evaluable a priori	Evaluable only a posteriori

These differences are the same as those discussed in the podcast (see slide 10 of podcast 3) but they are ordered differently and we are talking about validity now rather than 'truth-preservingness'.

We'll look at each of these differences in turn, picking up the vocabulary and distinctions we need en route.

Deductive Arguments Are Either Good or Bad

Deductive arguments are either good or bad. There is no 'in between'. Good deductive arguments are called 'valid', bad ones 'invalid'. Here are the definitions:

Def: **an argument is *valid* iff there is no logically possible situation in which all its premises are true and its conclusion false.**

Def: **an argument is *invalid* iff there is a logically possible situation in which all its premises are true and its conclusion false.**

These definitions make it clear that a deductive argument must be either valid or invalid. It must always be the case, mustn't it, that either:

- it *isn't* logically possible for all the premises of the argument to be true, yet the conclusion false

or

- it *is* logically possible for all the premises of the argument to be true yet the conclusion false?

In the first case the argument is valid. In the second case it is invalid. End of story. There is no 'in between'.

If we are to understand the notions of validity and invalidity, however, we shall have to learn about logical possibility and impossibility. We'll take a digression to do just that.

Empirical Versus Logical Possibility and Impossibility

Logical possibility is contrasted with *empirical* possibility. Here are the definitions:

> **Def:** something is *logically possible* iff it is consistent with the laws of logic as we currently understand them.

> **Def:** something is *empirically possible* iff it is consistent with the laws of nature as we currently understand them.

These notions are both defined in terms of *consistency*. In chapter two we looked at 'inconsistent terminology', where, in an argument different words with the same meaning were obscuring the clarity of an argument.

I said there that the terms 'consistent' and 'inconsistent' are ambiguous. In *this* use of the term 'consistent' and 'inconsistent' they are used not of 'terminology' but of *sentences.* Here are the definitions:

> **Def:** a set of sentences is *consistent* iff there is a logically possible situation in which all the sentences in the set can be true together.

> **Def:** a set of sentences is *inconsistent* iff there is no logically possible situation in which all the sentences in the set can be true together.

These definitions, together with the definitions of logical and empirical possibility imply that the laws of logic and the laws of nature are *sentences*. I will explain this below.

The notions of logical and empirical possibility are defined in terms of their consistency with *our current understanding* of the laws of logic and of nature. What does this mean?

Laws and Possibilities

Laws limit possibilities. The laws of nature limit what it is possible for a human being to do. In whatever we do, for example, we are limited by the fact we *cannot* travel faster than the speed of light.

The laws of the land limit only what it is possible to do *without risking judicial punishment*. We *can* violate the laws of the land. But in doing so, we risk punishment.

The laws of nature are not the ultimate limit to possibility. They *might*, after all, have been other than they are. There might be worlds where the laws of nature are different. These worlds are *possible,* but not *actual*.

In talking like this we are admitting another set of laws; the laws of logic. These govern which worlds *are* possible and which aren't. Something that is logically impossible, is impossible in *every* possible world. The laws of logic are the final limit on possibility.

Something that is empirically impossible is impossible only in *this* world. It is *logically possible*, therefore, that something should move faster than the speed of light, even if this is *empirically impossible.*

Kant believed that to violate the moral law is to violate the laws of logic. See http://plato.stanford .edu/entries/kant-moral/

Laws and Descriptions of Laws

Most people think the laws of logic and the laws of nature, unlike the laws of the land, exist independently of us; that they existed before we did and they will exist after we are gone. They govern us because they govern the world in which we live.

As curious creatures we attempt to describe our world. An important part of this is our attempt to describe the laws of nature and of logic.

But we must distinguish between the laws of logic and the laws of nature *as they are in themselves* and the laws of logic and the laws of nature *as we understand them to be at a given time.* This is a distinction between the *actual uniformities* of nature and of logic, and our *descriptions* of these uniformities.

In implying that laws are *sentences,* as I did above, I was, of course, talking of our *descriptions* of these laws rather than the laws themselves. Our descriptions of these laws are sentences (or more precisely sets of sentences).

This means that we must also distinguish between logical and empirical possibility and impossibility *as they are in themselves*, and the same notions *as we understand them to be at a given time.* We must also recognise the possibility that our understanding is not correct.

Let's see how this works in practice by discussing first *logical* possibility then *empirical* possibility.

95

Logical Impossibility

Logical impossibilities generate logical contradictions. Logical contradiction is a *rational* relation. It holds between two beliefs or between the sentences that express these beliefs. It can also hold of a single belief, or the sentence expressing it, when that belief contradicts *itself.*

The belief [squares are circular], for example, is self-contradictory. This means we are rationally obliged to reject it: it *cannot* be true. It is logically impossible for it to be true.

Its being self-contradictory seems to mean, in fact, that you can't even *hold* this belief. Try entertaining it and you will see what I mean.

This sort of psychological impossibility is evidence for a logical law. Something inconsistent with a law of nature seems perfectly thinkable. We don't have any problem entertaining the possibility, for example, that neutrinos travel faster than light. But it seems impossible even to *think* about logical impossibilities. At best we get an *illusion* of being able to grasp the concept of a square circle. This probably falls out of the fact that 'that circle is square' is syntactically correct.

But it is not *always* easy to say when we are faced with a logical contradiction.

Is it, for example, psychologically impossible to entertain the idea that you are a hippopotamus? It is undoubtedly *difficult* to think about being a hippopotamus. But does the idea generate a logical contradiction?

It is for *philosophers,* whose job it is to map the laws of logic, to ask what is and what isn't logically possible. That means we get to ask questions like 'could I be a hippopotamus?' Indeed someone *pays* us to think about such questions! (Not very much it must be admitted). In doing so we are constrained, of course, by the laws of logic.

Logical Possibility and the Actual World

Examples like the one about the hippopotamus get philosophers a bad name. You might even think such questions are a waste of time.

But mapping the laws of logic is important. The laws of logic determine which laws of nature are possible. Knowing what they are can save us a lot of trouble. *Nothing* logically impossible, after all, is empirically possible.

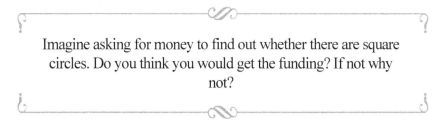

Imagine asking for money to find out whether there are square circles. Do you think you would get the funding? If not why not?

The fact that the belief [squares are circular] is self-contradictory means that circular squares *cannot* exist: they are logical impossibilities. Conclusions about *logical* possibilities can tell us something about *empirical* possibilities.

Again, though, this is not always easy. If you could travel back in time wouldn't you be able to kill one of your parents *before* you were conceived? If this is, as it seems, *logically* impossible, then time travel is ruled out by logic. Any attempt to show it is empirically possible will be a waste of time.

Yet physicist Michio Kaku argues that no law of *physics* precludes time travel: http://www.youtube.com/watch?v=X02WMNoHSm8 If, one day, physics shows time travel is *empirically* possible, then time travel *can't* be logically impossible.

The Usefulness of Contradiction

You might reasonably ask how, if it is psychologically impossible even to *think* about logical impossibilities, we can find ourselves in the situation described in the last two paragraphs. Doesn't the fact we can *think* about time travel show that time travel *is* logically possible?

Unfortunately it is not as simple as this. Whilst it doesn't seem psychologically possible to think something *self*-contradictory, it is certainly psychologically possible to hold two beliefs that contradict *each other*.

Here is such a pair of beliefs:

1. the Earth is round

2. it is not the case the Earth is round.

These sentences are contradictory. If one is true, the other *must* be false.

This 'must' is the must of *logical necessity*. Something is logically *necessary* if it is not logically possible for it *not* to be true; if it is true in *every* possible world.

But there is no *psychological* barrier to holding both these beliefs , at least until you *notice* that you hold both beliefs and that they contradict. Then it *will* become psychologically necessary for you to drop one of them (you cannot drop both *because* they are contradictories).

Thinking about time travel is like this. We *seem* to be able to think about it *until* we hit the logical contradiction.

Why Argument Works

That logical contradictions can go unnoticed explains why deduction works. When, often as a result of an argument, you notice you hold two beliefs that contradict each other, you are rationally obliged to drop one.

You might, of course, ignore the problem and hope it goes away (it won't). Lots of human beings choose not to exercise their capacity for reason, hating to change their minds or drop any of their beliefs. I assume, as you are reading this book, that you are not one of them!

It is not only logical contradictions that go unnoticed. We also miss the logical consequences of our beliefs. You noticed this, perhaps, in chapter one when you realised that you believe that zebras don't carry handbags.

That we often miss the logical consequences of our beliefs answers a question often posed about deduction: how can it teach us anything we don't already know?

The conclusion of a good deductive argument is a logical consequence of its premises. It tells us *nothing* that wasn't available to us in the premises. If you believe the premises of a valid argument, you must believe the conclusion. It is psychologically *necessary* to believe the conclusion because it is a logical consequence of the premises.

If you were ideally rational you would believe all the logical consequences of your beliefs. Deduction would be useless to you.

But we can be very bad at working out the logical consequences of our beliefs. Have a look at this argument:

Argument 3.3:

Premises one: All the world loves a lover

Premise two: Romeo loves Juliet

Conclusion: All the world loves Juliet.

Do you find this conclusion surprising? You shouldn't. If all the world loves a lover, and Romeo loves Juliet, then Juliet loves Romeo (because all the world *including Juliet* loves a lover). As *Juliet* is a lover, of course, all the world loves *her*. (I owe this example to Dr. Brian King, of Worcester College Oxford).

The conclusions of good deductive arguments can be surprising even though they tell us nothing we didn't – in a sense - already know.

Psychological necessity and impossibility are evidence – albeit inconclusive – for the laws of logic. But is our *current understanding* of the laws of logic the correct one?

The Laws of Logic and Our Understanding of Them

Findings in quantum mechanics are believed, by some philosophers, to suggest that we should drop the logical laws we know as 'the law of excluded middle' (it is always the case that either P or not P) and 'the law of double negation' (if it is not the case that not-P then it is the case that P). There are mathematicians (the Intuitionists) who believe the same thing.

The fact we *think* something is a logical law is not sufficient for it *actually* to be so. Our current understanding of the laws of logic might be incorrect.

This is not surprising. Why should beliefs about the laws of logic be the only beliefs that *can't* be incorrect?

This is why 'logical possibility' and 'logical impossibility' are both defined in relation to *our current* understanding of the laws of logic. We may not know whether in *actual* fact circular squares or married bachelors are logically impossible, but we do know that *relative to the current state of our knowledge* circular squares and married bachelors are logically impossible.

If you would like to learn more about how quantum mechanics and Intuitionistic Mathematics might affect our understanding of the laws of logic try this site:
http://plato.stanford.edu/entries/qt-quantlog/

http://plato.stanford.edu/entries/intuitionism/

Empirical Impossibility

Empirical possibility is not defined by appeal to the laws of logic , or, therefore, to *logical contradiction.* Empirical possibility is defined instead by appeal to the laws of *nature*, or rather to *our current understanding* of the laws of nature. Let's see why.

It is inconsistent with the laws of *nature,* as we currently understand them, that cats should talk intelligently about Kant or that pigs should fly. This means, according to our definitions, that it is *empirically impossible* both that cats should talk intelligently about Kant, or that pigs should fly.

Who knows, though, what biotechnology might come up with? We can already produce rabbits that glow in the dark and goats whose milk contains spider silk. Perhaps one day we will produce cats that talk intelligently about Kant, or pigs that can fly?

If you are interested in the biotechnological successes mentioned above you might like to check them out here:
http://www.newscientist.com/article/dn16-mutant-bunny.html
http://www.bbc.co.uk/news/science-environment-16554357

I have written a book on bioethics. You'll find it here: *http://amzn.to/118DJ3b* *and at* *http://www.cambridge.org/gb/academic/subjects/life-sciences/bioethics/bioethics-introduction*

The very possibility that we might actually produce intelligent talking cats or flying pigs demonstrates that there is no (obvious) *logical contradiction* generated by the idea of cats talking intelligently about Kant , or pigs flying. So it is consistent with our current understanding of the laws of logic that cats should talk intelligently about Kant, or that pigs should fly.

But neither of these situations is consistent with the laws of *nature* as we currently understand them.

Given our definitions, therefore, cats that talk intelligently about Kant and pigs that fly, are both *empirically impossible,* even if they are *logically* possible.

Exercise 3.2: Please say whether the following situations are logically possible, impossible or necessary, or empirically impossible, possible or necessary, or such that we can't tell:

1. The laws of nature might be different.

2. Mike Dando won the record for underwater swimming without breathing apparatus – he managed ten miles!

3. $2 + 2 = 5$.

4. That circle has four sides.

5. $5 + 7 = 12$.

6. Aged 57 Sheldon Cooper achieved his wish to travel in time.

7. Someone with the HD gene on chromosome four will get HD.

8. James was surprised, when he woke up, to find that he had turned into a frog.

Answers on page 364

That ends this lengthy digression on logical and empirical possibility and impossibility. Let's now return to the first characteristic that distinguishes deduction from induction: the fact that validity is an either/or matter but that, for an inductive argument, 'good' is a matter of degree.

Inductive Arguments Are Either Strong or Weak

Deductive arguments, if valid, *entail* their conclusions: it is logically impossible for their premises to be true and their conclusions false. If a deductive argument is *invalid*, on the other hand, there will be a logically possible situation in which its premises are true and its conclusion false. We can be certain, therefore, that if the premises of an argument entail its conclusion, the argument is a deductive one.

Inductive arguments, however, are *always* such that there is a logically possible situation in which their premises are true and their conclusions false. In chapter four we shall see that this is because all inductive arguments rely on the assumption that the future will be like the past. That the conclusion of an argument follows from its premises only on the assumption that the future will be like the past (i.e. that things will go on as before) is a major clue to the fact that an argument is inductive.

If we were to evaluate inductive arguments by the definition of 'good' used for deductive arguments there wouldn't *be* any good inductive arguments. But there *are* good inductive arguments, or at least there are inductive arguments that are better than other inductive arguments. Check out the two arguments below:

Argument 3.4:

Premise One: Last time I saw Marianne she was wearing a red dress

Conclusion: The next time I see Marianne she will be wearing a red dress.

Argument 3.5:

Premise one: The sun has risen every day in the whole history of the universe

Conclusion: The sun will rise tomorrow.

Argument 3.5 seems to be a much better argument than argument 3.4. Yet for each argument there is a possible situation in which the premises are true and the conclusion false. We'd have such a situation for argument 3.4 if Marianne was wearing green next time you saw her. We'd have such a situation for argument 3.5 if tonight the sun explodes.

Inductive arguments are never valid. But they don't have to be valid to be good. It suffices for an inductive argument to be good that the truth of its premises significantly raises the likelihood that the conclusion will also be true.

Argument 3.5 is such that the truth of its premises makes the truth of its conclusion hugely likely. The truth of the premises of argument 3.4, on the other hand, raises the likelihood of the truth of the conclusion only *very* slightly, if at all. Argument 3.5 is a *strong* inductive argument, argument 3.4 is a *weak* one.

Here are the definitions:

> **Def:**   **an inductive argument is *strong* iff the truth of all its premises significantly raises the likelihood that its conclusion will be true.**

> **Def:**   **an inductive argument is *weak* iff the truth of all its premises doesn't significantly raise the likelihood that its conclusion will be true.**

Whether the truth of a set of premises 'significantly raises the likelihood' of the truth of a conclusion or not is a *matter of degree*.

'Good' for an inductive argument is *not,* therefore, an either/or matter.

Exercise 3.3: Please say whether the following arguments are valid, invalid, strong or weak:

1. Audrey Hepburn was a great actor. All female actors, if they were great, were beautiful. Therefore Audrey Hepburn was beautiful.

2. The cat is genetically healthy, fed well, provided with water and treated with affection. Therefore the cat is thriving.

3. If the plant is treated well and given the right nutrients it will thrive. The plant is thriving. Therefore the plant is being treated well and given the right nutrients.

4. The man at the station, and the taxi driver, have both been wonderful. I am going to love everyone in this town.

Answers on page 365

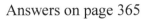

We can now proceed to the second characteristic that distinguishes deduction from induction

Deduction, Induction, Conclusivity and Certainty

With deduction, if an argument is valid, it will always be valid. Nothing could ever change it. A deductive argument, in other words, if valid, is *conclusively* valid. Deduction can give us *certainty*.

With induction, on the other hand, however strong or weak the argument it is *always* possible that we could learn something that would radically change our evaluation of the argument. Induction does *not* give us certainty; the evaluation of an inductive argument is never conclusive.

There are technical terms that capture this distinction. Deductive validity is *monotonic*, whereas inductive strength is *non-monotonic*.

Here are the definitions:

Def: **a property is *monotonic* iff it cannot be changed by the addition of new information.**

Def: **a property is *non-monotonic* iff it can be changed by the addition of new information.**

Deductive Validity is Monotonic

If an argument is valid, it will remain valid whatever else you might learn. Let's look at why this is so.

Consider argument 3.1 again:

Argument 3.1:

Premise one: If it is spring the snowdrops will be out

Premise two: It is spring

Conclusion: The snowdrops will be out.

To change this from a valid argument to an invalid argument we would have to bring about, by adding further premises, a possible situation in which the premises are all true and the conclusion *false*.

Add a True Premise

So imagine adding, to argument 3.1, another premise (any premise you like) that is true. Is that going to change the fact that the argument is valid (i.e. that there is no possible situation in which the premises are all true and the conclusion false)?

No, it isn't. We can't, by adding another true premise, produce a possible situation in which *the premises are all true and the conclusion false.* All we do is add another true premise.

Add a False Premise

Now imagine adding a false premise to argument 3.1 (again you can add any premise you like, including one that contradicts one of the existing premises). Does *this* change the argument from being a valid argument to being an invalid argument?

Again it would do this *only* if its addition would produce a possible situation in which all the premises are true and the conclusion false. But if the premise we have added is a false one, then it will *not* be the case that all the (new) premises are true. They *were* all true, before we added a false one. But now all *but one* will be true.

In both cases we have failed to produce a possible situation in which all the premises are true yet the conclusion false. Bivalence, however, tells us that in trying to change the validity of the argument by adding first a *true* premise, and second a *false* premise, we have covered all the bases. If, having tried both, we have failed to change the validity of the argument then that's it; it cannot be changed.

It is not possible to change a valid argument into an invalid one by the addition of further premises. Deductive validity is monotonic.

In the podcasts I had a bit of a brainstorm and gave the impression that *invalidity* is also monotonic. It isn't. We can, by adding new premises to an invalid argument, make it valid. It is only *validity* that is monotonic. We tried to edit the podcasts to remove the misleading things I said. I hope we succeeded. But if anyone was confused I apologise.

Inductive Strength is Non-Monotonic

Inductive strength, unlike deductive validity, is *non-monotonic*. This means that no matter how strong an inductive argument is, it is always possible for us to learn something that weakens it. It is also always possible we might learn something that strengthens a weak inductive argument.

In the podcasts (podcast 3, slide 45) I used the following example to show that a seemingly strong inductive argument can be seriously weakened by the addition of further information.

Argument 3.6:

Premise one: Jones confessed

Conclusion: Jones is guilty of the crime.

Argument 3.6 is a fairly strong inductive argument (given the suppressed premise 'those who confess to a crime are usually guilty of having committed the crime').

But now add:

Premise two: Ten independent witnesses testify to Jones being 100 miles away when the crime was committed

The argument is now extremely weak.

> *I adapted the examples in this section from some used by Mark Sainsbury in Logical Forms: An Introduction to Philosophical Logic (Blackwell, 1991) can be found at metafore.com/cr/ms*

In the podcasts (podcast 3, slide 46) I used this argument to demonstrate that an inductively weak argument can be changed into an inductively strong one:

Argument 3.7:

Premise one: Jones was present at the crime scene

Conclusion: Jones is guilty of the crime.

This is a pretty weak argument isn't it? But now add this premise:

Premise two: Smith, the policeman who tried to stop Jones kill the man, saw Jones plunge the dagger into the man's heart

Immediately the argument becomes pretty strong.

Inductive strength *can* be altered, therefore, by the acquisition of new information. This means that it is non-monotonic. The evaluation of an inductive argument is *never* conclusive, it *never* gives us certainty.

Exercise 3.4: Might the addition of further information change our minds about an evaluation of the following arguments:

1. Jane is a philosopher. All philosophers are poor. Therefore Jane is poor.

2. Tom is an oilman. 90% of oilmen are rich. Therefore Tom is rich.

3. Many students do well despite difficult backgrounds. Jaz has a difficult background. She could still do well.

Answers on page 365

Knowledge A Priori and A Posteriori

The third and final difference between deduction and induction is that whilst we can know *a priori* whether a deductive argument is valid or invalid, it is only ever possible to tell *a posteriori* whether an inductive argument is weak or strong.

Here are the two definitions you need:

Def: **to know something *a priori* is to know it without needing to bring to bear any background knowledge of the world.**

Def: **to know something *a posteriori* is to know it only having brought to bear some background knowledge of the world.**

You don't need to move from your armchair to tell me whether there are any square circles. You only have to reflect on your concept [square] and your concept [circle]. Your knowledge that circles can't be square is *a priori*. No empirical investigation is required to determine its truth value.

You would have to move from your armchair, though, to tell me how many white mugs there are on my desk. You can reflect on your concept of [white mug] and [desk] until the cows come home, you'll never learn how many white mugs there are on my desk. For this you have to conduct an empirical investigation: you'd have to *look* at my desk and *count* the white mugs. Knowledge of this kind is *a posteriori*.

You might object that, in order to reflect on your concepts of [square] and [circle], you *do* need background experience. How could you even *have* the concepts of [square] and [circle] without having *some* background knowledge of the world?

This is true. Indeed arguably you couldn't have the concepts of [square] and [circle] without having a language. Someone with a language must have a fairly significant amount of background information.

Nevertheless, once you have grasped the concepts of [square], [circle], and the concepts of logic, you have all you need to *determine the truth* of 'no circle is square'. You do not need *further* knowledge of the world. This is what makes the knowledge involved *a priori*.

If you'd like to learn more about a priori knowledge check out the Stanford Encyclopaedia's entry:
http://plato.stanford.edu/entries/apriori/

The Internet Encyclopaedia of Philosophy is good on this distinction:
http://www.iep.utm.edu/apriori/

Deductive Arguments Can Be Evaluated A Priori

So the third difference between deductive arguments and inductive arguments is that deductive arguments can be evaluated a priori. Inductive arguments can only ever be evaluated a posteriori.

To see this have another look at argument 3.1, remembering that it is a deductive argument:

Argument 3.1:

Premise one: If it is spring the snowdrops will be out

Premise two: It is spring

Conclusion: The snowdrops will be out.

The *content* of argument 3.1, the fact that it is about snowdrops and spring, is irrelevant to the question of whether its conclusion follows from its premises. Here is another argument with a completely different *content* but the same *form:*

Argument 3.8:

Premise one: If the litmus paper turns red the liquid is acidic

Premise two: The litmus paper turned red

Conclusion: The liquid is acidic.

The *content* of argument 3.8 is completely different from the content of argument 3.1. But the *structure* of argument 3.8 is the same as that of argument 3.1. Here is that structure:

Premise one: If P then Q

Premise two: P

Conclusion: Q.

The words 'form' and 'structure' are interchangeable. Both refer to what is left of an argument once its content is stripped away, leaving only the logical words (in this case 'if/then'), and the logical relation between premises and conclusion (the fact that the same sentences appear in different places).

> To read about the distinction between form and content check out this entry in the Stanford Encyclopaedia of Philosophy:
> http://plato.stanford.edu/entries/logical-constants/

Arguments one and eight are both deductive arguments of the sub-type *modus ponens* (in Latin 'mode that affirms'). Any argument of this form, *whatever its content*, will be valid. The minute you see this structure, it doesn't matter what the argument is about, it will be valid.

By the same token it is always possible to tell that a deductive argument is bad, again just by looking at its structure. Here is an example of the fallacy of *affirming the consequent:*

Argument 3.9:

Premise one: If it is spring the snowdrops will be out

Premise two: The snowdrops are out

Conclusion: It is spring.

Argument 3.9 has the structure:

Premise one: If P then Q

Premise two: Q

Conclusion: P.

Just as any example of *modus ponens* is a *good* deductive argument, any example of *affirming the consequent*, any argument with *this* structure, is a *bad* deductive argument, *whatever* its content

The content of a deductive argument is irrelevant to its evaluation. This is what makes the evaluation of a deductive argument *a priori*. You don't need to know anything about the subject matter of a deductive argument in order to evaluate it.

Deduction is 'topic-neutral'. It doesn't matter what you are talking about, or even how much you know about it, you will *always* be able to tell whether a deductive argument is good or bad simply by appeal to its structure. Evaluating deductive arguments is the ultimate transferrable skill!

In chapter 5 I will be introducing the notion of an 'interpretation'. An interpretation allows us to 'strip the content' from an argument thereby displaying its structure. I have just used Ps and Qs to do this to arguments eight and nine. Interpretations are allocations of 'sentence letters' (letters that stand for sentences) to the sentences of an argument. All interpretations are argument-specific as you can see from the fact that the interpretation for arguments eight and nine are:

Interpretation for argument 3.8:

P: The litmus paper turns red
Q: The liquid is acidic

Interpretation for argument 3.9:

P: It is spring
Q: The snowdrops are out

I have set out both interpretations according to convention. This requires us to put a sentence letter (a capital letter like P, Q, R, S, T,...etc), followed by a colon (:) followed by the sentence for which the sentence letter will stand as we analyse *this* argument. So the sentence letter 'P' stands for 'the litmus paper turns red' in argument 3.8, but in argument 3.9 the same sentence letter ('P') stands for 'it is spring'. Please note that *all* the sentences used in an interpretation must be declarative sentences (see chapter one, page 26).

Exercise 3.5: Can you evaluate this as a good or bad argument despite the fact you have no idea what it is talking about?

Premise one: If widgets are holomo, then widgets are tralem

Premise two: This widget is not tralem

Conclusion: This widget is not holomo.

Answers on page 366

Inductive Arguments Can Only Ever Be Evaluated A Posteriori

Inductive arguments cannot be evaluated a priori. They can only ever be evaluated a posteriori. Look again at:

Argument 3.2:

Premise one: Everyone with Huntington's Disease ever genetically tested has had the HD gene on chromosome 4

Premise two: Freya has HD and is about to be genetically tested

Conclusion: Freya will be found to have the HD gene on chromosome four.

We have considered the possibility that there is a genetic variant of HD, so Freya might have this other kind. But are there other possibilities we need to consider in evaluating this argument?

What if I were to ask you how many people with HD had been genetically tested? How secure would be the claim that the conclusion of this argument follows from its premises if it turned out that only 3 people with HD, out of the thousands of people with HD, had ever been genetically tested?

It is not *just* your understanding of logical form (or structure) that enables you to evaluate an inductive argument. You must also know something about the world. Specifically you must know something about what the argument is *about*, about the subject matter of the argument, about its *content*.

Empirical knowledge, of some kind, is essential to the evaluation of inductive arguments. They can only ever be evaluated *a posteriori.*

Distinguishing Deduction and Induction

So the three characteristics that distinguish deduction from induction are:

- deductive arguments are either valid or invalid, whilst inductive arguments are strong or weak to some degree;

- deductively valid arguments are monotonic , whilst inductive arguments are non-monotonic (we might change our evaluation of them on acquiring more information);

- deductive arguments can be evaluated a priori, whilst inductive arguments can only ever be evaluated a posteriori.

I have treated these three characteristics in the order given here. If, however, you are trying to decide whether an argument is deductive or inductive, it is often the final characteristic that will help you most. This is especially true if the argument is a complicated one.

Complicated arguments almost always have to be analysed before you can do anything else. Until the irrelevancies, inconsistent terms and cross references have been removed we often can't see the argument for words (if you see what I mean).

But once we *have* analysed an argument, it can be quite easy to identify its constituent sentences, provide an interpretation for them and decide whether the structure might, on its own, enable you to evaluate the argument.

Exercise 3.6: Are the following arguments inductive or deductive?

1. "It has so far been observed that thousands of babies born with trisomy 21 (henceforth T21) have Down's Syndrome (henceforth DS) and that no baby born with T21 does not have DS. The next baby born with T21 will therefore have DS."

2. "If thousands of babies born with T21 have DS and no baby born with T21 does not have DS, then there is a causal law relating T21 and DS. If there is a causal law relating T21 and DS then T21 necessitates DS. If T21 *necessitates* DS then it is not possible that a baby should be born with T21 but *not* DS. If thousands of babies born with T21 have DS and no baby born with T21 does not have DS, then it is not possible that a baby should be born with T21 but *not* DS.*"

Answers on page 367

Abductive Arguments

There are people (lots of them) who believe that abductive arguments are a third category of argument, neither deductive nor inductive.

An abductive argument is an *inference to the best explanation*. It has the form:

Given evidence E and candidate explanations $H_1,\ldots, H_n$ of E, infer the truth of *that* H_i which best explains E.

Informally this reads that if we have several hypotheses $(H_1,\ldots, H_n)$ by which to explain a given set of observations or evidence (E), we should accept as true that hypothesis that explains E best.

We use this sort of argument every time we believe something someone tells us. If Sue, for example, tells us that *Amour* is on at the local cinema and on this basis we make plans to see it, we are relying on an argument that goes something like:

Argument 3.10:

Premise one: Sue says *Amour* is on at the local cinema

Premise two: The best explanation of Sue's saying that *Amour* is on at the local cinema is that *Amour* is on at the local cinema

Conclusion: *Amour* is on at the local cinema.

Abduction appears to be a crucial part of the scientific method. For example when, in the nineteenth century Neptune was discovered, this was made possible by an argument that went something like:

Argument 3.11:

Premise one: The Planet Uranus departs from the orbit predicted by Newton's theory of universal gravitation

Premise two: The best explanation of Uranus's deviant orbit is the existence of an as yet undiscovered eighth planet

Conclusion: There is an as yet undiscovered eighth planet.

Another possible explanation, of course, for Uranus's deviant orbit, was that Newton's theory of universal gravitation was false. But this seemed less likely to be true than that another planet should exist. This abductive argument justified the expenditure of much time, money and energy in the attempt – successful – to discover Neptune, the eighth planet.

Abduction as a form of induction

Abduction turns on the notion of the *best* explanation. In choosing which hypothesis is the one to accept, we assume that explanations differ in value, and choose one of our candidate explanations as the 'best'.

Dimensions of theory or hypothesis evaluation have been thought to include the following:

- simplicity;

- pragmatic success;

- scope;

- integration into the rest of contemporary knowledge.

So the idea is that the hypothesis that best satisfies these (or some sub-set) of such criteria is the one we should choose.

But whichever dimension of evaluation we are looking at, we seem to be reasoning that theories satisfying this criterion have worked in the past, so such theories will work again in the future. This strikes me as clearly an inductive inference. It relies on our current understanding of the laws of nature, it is non-monotonic (we might learn something to change our minds about this being the best explanation), and it is probabilistic (we can never be *certain* that an explanation is the best one).

You might, of course, having read some of the references supplied above, disagree with me and insist that abduction isn't a form of inductive inference. Nevertheless, in this book, we shall treat it as such. In chapter four, for example, when we consider the evaluation of inductive arguments, we shall treat abduction as a sub-type of induction.

Let's now test what we have learned in this chapter:

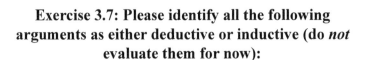

Exercise 3.7: Please identify all the following arguments as either deductive or inductive (do *not* evaluate them for now):

1. The birds on my bird table are brown. Sparrows are brown. Therefore the birds on my bird table are sparrows.

2. The weather forecast tells us that snow is on the way. It is likely, therefore, that snow is on the way.

3. Teachers are kind souls. Kind souls don't shout at children. Therefore teachers do not shout at children.

4. Nearly all Texans are rich. Bill is a Texan, therefore, Bill is rich.

5. The Cypriot government is making a raid on residents' savings. This may lead to riots.

6. Jean is a smoker, John exercises daily. Therefore John is likely to live longer than Jean.

Answers on page 368

At the beginning of this chapter you were told that by the end you would be able to:

- distinguish between arguments that are good and arguments that are sound;

- say what is involved in a conclusion following from a set of premises;

- describe two types of 'following from' deductive and inductive;

- explain the difference between logical and empirical possibility;

- explain why deduction is an either/or matter, whilst induction is a matter of degree;

- explain what is meant by 'deduction gives us certainty, induction only probability';

- explain why good deductive arguments are conclusive, inductive argument not;

- explain the notions of 'a priori'and 'a posteriori';

- explain what it is to evaluate arguments a priori and a posteriori.

Can you do these things? If so well done! If not, you'll certainly find it worth your while to go back to the sections covering the things of which you are uncertain and get them under your belt before you continue.

You've now finished chapter three!

CHAPTER FOUR

Evaluating Inductive Arguments

This chapter corresponds to the *fifth* podcast in my series: **Critical Reasoning: A Romp Through The Foothills of Logic.** The video podcast can be found at metafore.com/CR4video, the audio-only podcast at metafore.com/CR4audio, slides at metafore.com/CR4slides and a transcript at http://mariannetalbot.co.uk/transcripts/.

Podcast Warning: In writing the book I decided that it would be better to tackle the evaluation of inductive arguments before the evaluation of deductive arguments. This reverses the order of the podcasts So the podcast for this fourth chapter really is podcast FIVE not FOUR.

In chapter three we learned that an argument is good only if its conclusion follows from its premises. In chapter five we shall be learning a systematic method for evaluating deductive arguments. In this chapter we shall only consider how to evaluate inductive arguments.

There is no systematic method for evaluating inductive arguments. This is true even when an inductive argument is based on the best statistical methods, and involves the best that probability theory has to offer. Statistics and probability theory are both formal mathematical theories. I shall indicate when these are relevant, but as this is an introduction to *informal* logic, we shan't dwell on either.

In this chapter we shall examine *why* inductive arguments never deliver certainty. Then we'll consider whether induction is inferior to deduction. Finally we shall list the different types of inductive argument, together with the questions needed to evaluate each.

A careful reading of this chapter will ensure you are able to:

- explain why induction relies on the Principle of the Uniformity of Nature (PUN);

- show that the PUN cannot be justified;

- argue for the claim that induction is non-rational;

- explain the paradoxes of confirmation;

- explain why auxiliary assumptions are required;

- understand why Popper argued that scientists never use induction;

- evaluate Popper's argument;

- explain the arguments for and against the idea that induction is inferior to deduction;

- enumerate the different types of inductive argument;

- list the questions needed to evaluate each kind of inductive argument.

As usual, at the end of the chapter you'll have an opportunity to check that you *have* understood all this.

Why Induction Is Never Conclusive

Inductive arguments cannot deliver certainty. This is because they rely on something the Scottish philosopher David Hume called *the Principle of the Uniformity of Nature* (PUN). The PUN is the assumption that the future will be like the past.

Take this argument:

Argument 4.1:

Premise one: The left side of the patient's face has fallen, his left arm is weak and his speech is slurred

Premise two: The best explanation of this combination of symptoms is that the patient is having, or has had, a stroke

Conclusion: The patient is having, or has had, a stroke.

The second premise of this argument relies on the fact that because, *in the past,* people whose faces have dropped, whose arms are weak and whose speech is slurred have often turned out to have had, or be having, a stroke, this *current* person, who manifests the same symptoms, is probably also having, or has had, a stroke. Here we see the PUN in use.

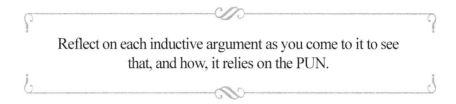

Reflect on each inductive argument as you come to it to see
that, and how, it relies on the PUN.

The PUN and Expectations

Hume knew things can happen unexpectedly. The future is not
always like the past. Any prediction we make on this assumption
might fail. Even if the sun has risen every single day in the
history of the universe, tomorrow it might *not* rise. Even the
strongest inductive argument is such that its premise(s) might be
true yet its conclusion false.

Our expectations are regularly unfulfilled. Despite this we
continue to think nature is uniform. We explain the events that
surprise us in terms of the interactions between the natural
uniformities that we continue to think of as governing our world.

> *You can learn more about Hume here:*
> *http://plato.stanford.edu/entries/hume/ or here:*
> *http://www.youtube.com/watch?*
> *v=ET9oRKEwESA*

Hume and Natural Necessity

Hume believed that when we predict A will follow B on the basis
of observing correlations between As and Bs; our observations
have set up in us a mental *habit*. We now *expect* A to follow B.

Hume argued that 'natural necessity' is nothing more than this expectation. Many modern philosophers, though, deny that the laws of nature are just habits of *ours.*

Even so we have to agree with Hume in recognising that our only *evidence* for the laws of nature consists in our observation of correlations, and that this evidence is not conclusive, not least because it relies on the PUN.

Justifying the Principle of the Uniformity of Nature

It is impossible to justify the PUN. There is no good argument for believing that the future will be like the past.

Deduction won't work. No logical contradiction is generated by supposing that the future will *not* be like the past.

Induction won't work either. To claim that the future will be like the past in the future because the future has always been like the past in the past is to argue in a circle. In chapter five we'll see that circular arguments are *valid.* But they are not persuasive.

Exercise 4.1: Can you work out, from the definition of validity, why circular arguments (arguments the conclusions of which are amongst their premises) are valid but not persuasive?

Answer on page 369

Induction and Non-Rationality

Hume argued that we do not engage in induction for *reasons*. It is, according to Hume, simply what human beings *do*. We might say that our brains are wired up to do it.

If we have evolved in a world governed by the PUN this would make sense. Perhaps the best explanation of our engaging in inductive inference is that nature *is* uniform? The assumption on which induction rests might, therefore, be *true*. But this doesn't mean is it *justified* (or even *justifiable*).

But doesn't this call into question the justification of science? After all, induction is at the core of scientific thinking. How can science be paradigmatically rational if at its core is faith in an assumption that *can't* be justified?

Science doesn't rely on faith in *God*, of course, only faith in the PUN. And science isn't *irrational* only *non-rational*. (Only rational things can be *irrational*.)

Even so, the fact that the PUN grounds all scientific thinking does mean that science relies on faith of some sort, and that it has at its core an assumption that can't be rationally justified.

Hume's problem is a major one.

Induction and Confirmation

Hume's is only the first problem that besets induction. The second, the 'paradox of ravens', was devised by Carl Hempel (see: http://plato.stanford.edu/entries/hempel/). This seems to force us to choose between three beliefs, each of which *seems* true. One of them is a belief about what counts as evidence *confirming* our hypotheses.

We take repeated observations of As being B as evidence for a hypothesis to the effect that *all* (or *most*) As are B. We then take further observations of As being B as evidence *confirming* this hypothesis (to some small degree).

So imagine every raven you have ever seen has been black. You will formulate the hypothesis 'all ravens are black'. You will then take new observations of black ravens to support your hypothesis.

A white raven will be evidence against your hypothesis. It demands the modification or rejection of the hypothesis. An obvious modification is: 'all *normal* ravens are black'.

This seems a sensible way to proceed even if it does rely on the PUN. It is certainly the way we *do* proceed. But there is a logical problem with this process.

The Paradox of Ravens

The hypothesis 'all ravens are black' is logically equivalent to the hypothesis 'all non-black things are non-ravens'. This falls out of the definition of 'logical equivalence':

> **Def:** two sentences are *logically equivalent* to each other if they are true and false in *exactly* the same conditions.

If 'all ravens are black' is true, 'all non-black things are non-ravens' *must* be true. If one sentence is false they must *both* be false. This 'must' is logical. A contradiction is generated by assuming 'all ravens are black' is true but 'all non-black things are non-ravens' is false or vice versa.

Next we need the 'Equivalence Principle':

EP: if evidence confirms a given hypothesis it also confirms any logically equivalent hypothesis.

132

This is straightforward. If two sentences are true and false under *exactly* the same conditions (and we know this) how could anything confirm (or falsify) one, but not the other?

But at this point the paradox emerges:

Argument 4.2:

Premise one: The sighting of a white gym shoe confirms 'all non-black things are non-ravens'

Premise two: 'All non-black things are non-ravens' is logically equivalent to 'all ravens are black'

Premise three: If evidence, e, confirms a given hypothesis it also confirms any logically equivalent hypothesis

Conclusion: The sighting of a white gym shoe confirms 'all ravens are black'.

This deductive argument is valid. To reject the conclusion we must reject one of the premises.

We *should* reject the conclusion – it would be daft to go looking for white gym shoes in order to confirm 'all ravens are black'. So which premise should we reject?

Premises two and three are logically unquestionable. But to reject premise one would be to reject the idea that a hypothesis is confirmed by its instances. But if so, what *does* confirm a hypothesis? How should we evaluate the truth of an inductive inference *except* against its instances?

Confirmation to a Tiny Degree

Any *single* observation, even of a black raven, confirms our hypothesis only to a tiny degree. Perhaps we could accept that the sighting of a white gym shoe also confirms it, perhaps to an even *smaller* degree?

But do observations of white gym shoes confirm 'all ravens are black' to *any* degree? Practically speaking, surely, the answer is 'no'?

Before we look at what is going wrong let's examine a third problem for induction.

Can you say what is going wrong here?

Induction and Hypothesis Choice

The third problem was identified by philosopher Nelson Goodman in Fact, Fiction and Forecast pages 72-80 (4th Edition Harvard University Press, 1983). This is available on Amazon here:

http://www.amazon.com/gp/product/0674290712

It is also available freely online here:

metafore.com/cr/ng

The third problem is known as the 'Grue Paradox' (or 'The New Riddle of Induction'). This questions the way we *choose* hypotheses.

Consider this inductive argument:

Argument 4.3:

Premise one: Repeated observations of green emeralds (and no observations of non-green emeralds) justify forming the hypothesis 'all emeralds are green'

Premise two: Many green emeralds have been seen

Conclusion: We are justified in forming the hypothesis 'all emeralds are green'.

Goodman questions this by inventing a new predicate 'grue'. He defines it thus:

Def: **something is *grue* if it is green and observed or blue and unobserved.**

(I have left out, as unnecessary, the time predicate that Goodman included in this definition). But once we have the predicate 'grue' argument 4.4 seems as acceptable as argument 4.3:

Argument 4.4:

Premise one: Repeated observations of grue emeralds (and no observations of non-grue emeralds) justify forming the hypothesis 'all emeralds are grue'

Premise Two: Many grue emeralds have been seen

Conclusion: We are justified in forming the hypothesis 'all emeralds are grue'.

The hypothesis 'all emeralds are grue' is now as justifiable as 'all emeralds are green'. Isn't it?

If not, why not?

How can we justify preferring the hypothesis 'all emeralds are green' to 'all emeralds are grue' when we have not - and never shall have - the slightest idea what unobserved emeralds look like?

The problem is not the introduction of a new predicate. We do this all the time. The verb 'to surf the web' was unknown in the 1950s.

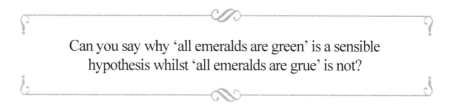

Can you say why 'all emeralds are green' is a sensible
hypothesis whilst 'all emeralds are grue' is not?

Dissolving the Paradoxes

Can you dissolve the paradoxes? If so I am impressed. If not you
won't be alone. In each case the solution lies in the importance of
background information, the so-called 'auxiliary assumptions'.

Whenever we formulate a hypothesis on the basis of evidence, and
whenever we decide what counts as evidence for or against a
hypothesis, we make use of auxiliary assumptions. We are often
unaware of this.

Let's consider this for each paradox.

(i) The Raven Paradox

In claiming that the sighting of a black raven confirms 'all ravens
are black', but that the sighting of a white gym shoe doesn't, we
rely on our belief that there are more non-black, non-ravens than
black ravens.

Imagine there are only 11 objects (one of which is you). Further
imagine that you know that, apart from yourself, there are nine
ravens and nine black things. The sighting of a white gym shoe
now *conclusively* confirms 'all ravens are black' doesn't it?

In the *actual* world, though, it would be daft to suppose the former
confirms the latter. Knowing this we reject the claim that a white
gym shoe could confirm 'all ravens are black'. So far as *logic* is
concerned, though, a white gym shoe is just as good a confirming
instance.

Interesting, isn't it, to see how oblivious we are to our reliance on background information?

(ii) The Grue Paradox

It seems obvious that we justifiably form the hypothesis 'all emeralds are green' on the basis of observing emeralds. But, given the definition of grue, why aren't we just as justified in forming the hypothesis 'all emeralds are grue'?

It is because we have smuggled into our choice of hypothesis an auxiliary assumption: *observing emeralds does not change their colour*. It is this, not logic, that makes us reject the hypothesis 'all emeralds are grue', in favour of 'all emeralds are green'.

> *To read about Grue, start with Goodman (ibid), then go to Frank Jackson , "Grue," Journal of Philosophy , lxxii, 5 (March 13, 1975):113–31.*
>
> *Here is a collection of solutions proposed over the forty years since Goodman proposed the problem: Douglas Stalker, ed., Grue! (Chicago: Open Court , 1994, available here: http://www.opencourtbooks.com/books_n/grue.htm*

Auxiliary Hypotheses

We cannot test a hypothesis without simultaneously testing numerous auxiliary assumptions; that the equipment is working properly, that the theory of gravity applies, that observing gem stones doesn't change their colour, or that there are more non-black non-ravens than black ravens.

The Grue paradox suggests we cannot even *choose* a hypothesis without relying on such assumptions. Yet we are often unaware of these auxiliary assumptions. We think – wrongly - it is pure *logic* that takes us from evidence to inference.

> *Here is a hugely influential paper on The Duhem-Quine thesis , which states the need for auxiliary assumptions:*
> *http://www.ditext.com/quine/quine.html*

The Status of Induction

We now have several reasons for saying induction is inferior to deduction:

- deduction gives certainty, induction only probability;

- deduction gives conclusive knowledge, induction is never conclusive;

- we can systematically evaluate deductive arguments but not inductive arguments;

- induction is grounded on faith in the PUN, deduction is not;

- induction relies on auxiliary assumptions, deduction does not.

Surely, therefore, induction *is* inferior to deduction?

Karl Popper and the Rejection of Induction

Believing this, and believing science to be paradigmatically rational, Karl Popper insisted that science does *not* rely on induction.

Rejecting the claim that we use induction to infer hypotheses from repeated observations, he argued that the process of scientific *discovery* is pure *conjecture*. Rejecting the claim that we confirm a hypothesis by observing instances of it, he insisted that we do not confirm hypotheses *at all*. Instead we *falsify* them. Falsification relies solely on *deduction*.

The raven hypothesis, for example, would be falsified by observations confirming premise two of this deductive argument:

Argument 4.5:

Premise one: 'All ravens are black' is false if there is even *one* non-black raven

Premise two: There is a non-black raven

Conclusion: The hypothesis 'all ravens are black' is false.

Popper's argument for the process of 'conjecture and refutation' was, in his day, hugely influential. Nevertheless it is unsound.

If you would like to read more about Popper's views try:
http://plato.stanford.edu/entries/popper/

Falsification is Important But Not All-Important

Falsification *is* important. Unless we can say what it would be for a theory to be false, we don't know how to *test* that theory. It is reasonably thought to be a necessary condition of calling a theory 'scientific', therefore, that it be falsifiable.

But if scientists always rejected a theory on discovering falsifying evidence, many useful scientific theories would have been rejected years ago. We would, for example, have rejected Newtonian mechanics on discovering that the orbit of Uranus deviated from the orbit predicted for it by this theory.

Instead it was suggested that we reject the auxiliary assumption that no as-yet-undiscovered planet was exerting a gravitational pull on Uranus. Neptune was discovered in 1846: http://www-history.mcs.st-and.ac.uk/HistTopics/ Neptune_and_Pluto.html

Popper's later theories addressed this problem, but philosophers disagree about whether he has succeeded in saving his theory.

Is Induction Inferior to Deduction?

Here are five reasons for denying that induction is inferior to deduction:

(a) We Cannot *Not* Use Induction

Deduction tells us only about what is *logically necessary*. It takes things we already know and generates their logical consequences. It adds *nothing*. It is because we are not perfectly rational that the conclusion of a deductive argument can surprise us.

Induction is *ampliative.* It amplifies and generalises our experience. It is only induction that enables us to diagnose illnesses, decide who was guilty, predict the discovery of the Higg's Boson or tomorrow's weather. Our interest in such contingent facts makes our use of induction non-negotiable.

(b) Induction Is As 'Certain' As Deduction.

Here are two arguments:

Argument 4.6:

Premise one: All ravens are black

Conclusion: If there is a raven at the gate of the Tower of London, it will be black.

Argument 4.7:

Premise one: All ravens so far observed have been black

Conclusion: If there is a raven at the gate of the Tower of London, it will be black.

Argument 4.6 is a valid deductive argument. If its premise is true, its conclusion *must* be true. Argument 4.7 is a strong inductive argument. Its premise might be true and its conclusion false. It clearly relies on the PUN.

The claim 'all ravens are black' must, however, be inductively based. It relies on the PUN just as clearly as the conclusion of argument 4.7 does. Our uncertainty about the truth of the inductive conclusion, therefore, is mirrored in our uncertainty about the truth of the deductive premise. This is true of *all* deductive arguments, not just those with inductive premises.

(c) Deduction is Also Grounded on 'Faith'

Induction is grounded on the PUN, which is unjustifiable. But how would we justify the rules of deduction?

Induction is too weak. Even if we have observed that whenever the premises of a valid argument are true, so is the conclusion, this doesn't justify our claiming this will *always* be the case.

But if we use *deduction* to justify deduction we'd argue in a circle wouldn't we?

The problem of justifying deduction seems exactly analogous to the problem of justifying induction.

(d) Deduction Only Takes Us So Far

On discovering Uranus's deviating orbit, we might have rejected Newtonian mechanics. Instead we questioned an auxiliary assumption: that no planet was exerting a gravitational pull on Uranus. We had presumably already rejected the possibility that our calculations were incorrect.

Faced with a valid argument we can *choose* to accept or reject its conclusion. If we reject the conclusion, we must reject a premise. But again we *choose* which premise to reject.

These choices will often be based on *inductive* reasoning.

When Mrs Thatcher, Britain's first female Prime Minister, was first in the British Cabinet it was said she was 'the best man in the cabinet'.

This seems to have been the reasoning:

Premise one: All women are passive

Premise two: Mrs. Thatcher is a woman

Sub-Conclusion: Mrs. Thatcher is passive.

Premise three: Mrs. Thatcher is *not* passive

Final Conclusion: Mrs. Thatcher is *not* a woman.

I found this 'joke' vaguely insulting. It was also made of Indira Ghandi who was said to be the *only* man in the (Indian) Cabinet! Perhaps I am over-sensitive? It undoubtedly illustrates the fact we have a choice of which premise to reject.

(e) For Practical Purposes Induction *Can* Yield Certainty

If you have the HD gene on chromosome four, there is a *logical* possibility, but no *empirical* possibility, that you won't develop Huntington's Disease. Given the laws of genetics, HD will *always* develop if someone with the HD gene lives long enough.

We *trust* our understanding of the laws of nature. We don't waste time worrying whether the water in the kettle will boil. Nor, when we send Curiosity to Mars or build the Large Hadron Collider, do we worry about anything other than whether our calculations are correct.

Natural necessity differs from logical necessity. But it is still a form of necessity.

Induction is Different Not Inferior

I hope you agree we can safely reject the idea that induction is inferior to deduction?

Induction is simply *different*. It differs in the characteristics outlined in chapter three, in being based on the PUN, and in relying on auxiliary assumptions.

All these characteristics contribute to there being no systematic method for evaluating inductive arguments. But this doesn't make induction inferior.

Armed with this reassurance, let's have look at what *can* be said about evaluating inductive arguments.

> *If you'd like to read more about the problem of induction, and philosophers' responses to it try: http://plato.stanford.edu/entries/induction-problem/*

Evaluating Inductive Arguments

Here are the five types of inductive argument I identified in podcast five, slide 22:

- inductive generalisations;

- causal generalisations;

- abductive arguments;

- arguments from analogy;

- arguments from authority.

We'll look at the key characteristics of each, and discuss the questions we need to answer to evaluate them effectively.

Are The Premises True?

We must always ask, of any inductive argument as with any other argument, whether its premises are true. The premises of an inductive argument will cite experiences, observations or experiments as evidence for the truth of the argument's conclusion.

Most of our inductions are informal, spontaneous and unconscious. When you go to *that* cupboard for *that* cereal it is because the cereal is *usually* in that cupboard, and because you *usually* enjoy the cereal. Life is full of unnoticed inductions.

Sometimes, though, we will intentionally:

- set out to find evidence for and/or against a hypothesis;

- think carefully about the experiences, observations and experiments that constitute evidence for or against our hypothesis;

- record our data as objectively, completely and correctly as possible.

If our premises have been arrived at by the use of well-tested statistical tools, carefully applied with the intention of providing evidence for or against a clear and plausible hypothesis we will, and should, have more faith in their truth than if they resulted from casual observation.

But the premises of an inductive argument will support its conclusion only if the conclusion *follows from* the premises. Our aim below is to identify which questions we need to ask, of inductions of each type, to decide whether its premises are true, and its conclusion follows.

Inductive Generalisation (Or Induction by Enumeration)

Here are two inductive generalisations:

Argument 4.8:

Premise one: Every time Lev has rung BT it has taken them ages to answer

Conclusion: When Sam rings BT it will take them ages to answer.

Argument 4.9:

Premise one: 93% of schoolchildren in the UK attend a state school

Premise two Jocasta is a schoolchild in the UK

Conclusion: The school Jocasta attends is a state school.

People once believed that all induction moved from 'the particular' to 'the general'. That this is false is demonstrated by argument 4.9 which moves from the general to the particular. Argument 4.8 too, seems to move from one particular to another (though arguably it must do so via a highly general premise such as 'it always takes BT ages to answer'.

Argument 4.8 takes us from a claim about sample of a population (calls Lev has made to BT) to a claim about another sample (Sam's calls to BT). In evaluating this argument we are interested in whether we are justified in thinking BT will take ages to answer Sam's call *given that* BT (apparently) took ages to answer Lev's calls.

Argument 4.9 takes us from a claim about a population to a claim about a member of that population. In evaluating it we are interested in whether we are justified in thinking that Jocasta goes to a state school *given that* she is a UK schoolchild and 93% of UK schoolchildren (by premise one) go to state schools. Let's compare these two arguments.

Objectivity in Data Collection

Lev might be an impatient person. Maybe, by Lev's lights, BT *has* always taken ages to answer him. But maybe we'd be surprised by BT's quick response?

In argument 4.9 did the '93%' come from websites devoted to either abolishing or arguing for independent education? Did it come from the government? Did I make it up? Positive answers might trigger suspicion about this figure.

Facts and figures often depend on definitions. The UK government counts 'free schools' and 'academies' as state schools. Others might see them as independent.

Premises might be true, in other words, *only* on a given understanding of them. If this understanding is questioned, the premises can be questioned.

Sample Sizes

Maybe Lev has only tried to ring BT twice? If so, even if we agree they have taken ages to answer, the sample is too small to generalise.

But *when* is a sample large enough?

People who are inductively bold will extrapolate from a sample that the inductively timid would reject as too small. Sample size is often a matter of judgement.

But if Lev has tried to ring BT *20* times, we can be more confident there is a pattern, that Lev hasn't just been unlucky.

Sample sizes don't have to represent particular percentages of a population (unless that population is very small). They need only be large enough to ensure findings are not distorted by *chance.*

Professional opinion pollsters rely on polls of 1000 people, a very small percentage of the voting population. Yet such polls are reasonably accurate. This is because any properly randomised sample of 1000 people is likely, roughly speaking, to share the views of any other properly randomised sample of 1000 people.

There are mathematical formulae for working out the sample sizes you would need to gain a certain level of confidence (say 95%) with a given margin of error (say plus or minus 5%). You can read about them here
http://www.osra.org/itlpj/bartlettkotrlikhiggins.pdf

Why should a population's being *small* mean that a sample must be a reasonable percentage of it to be large enough?

Answers on page 369

Representativeness of the Sample

If Lev has always tried to ring BT at 9am on Monday (when BT is busy), or 2pm on a Sunday (when fewer staff are on duty), this may reduce our confidence in argument 4.8. Perhaps BT answers with alacrity when fully staffed or less busy?

In argument 4.9 evaluating the argument depends more on whether *Jocasta* is representative of UK schoolchildren. If Jocasta is the child of a millionaire, the Headteacher of an independent school, or well-known advocates of home-schooling, she might not be.

> *You can read here about a classic example of bias in the choice of a sample:*
> *http://www.math.upenn.edu/~deturck/m170/wk4/lecture/case1.html*

Representativeness works both ways. Whether we are arguing from a sample to a population or from a population to a sample the sample must be representative of the population.

Exercise 4.3: "Drugs! Everyone does them, but
which ones do you do?"

This invited responses to a survey aimed at discovering how
many UK university students use controlled drugs.

Do you think those responding were likely to be representative
of UK university students?

Answers on page 370

Questions About Inductive Generalisations

Here is a list of the questions by which to evaluate inductive
generalisations (these are slightly different from those I gave on
slide 33 of podcast five):

1. Are the premises true?

2. Was the evidence recorded objectively?

3. Are we arguing from a large enough sample?

4. Is the sample we are arguing from, or to, representative of
   the population?

Exercise 4.4: Evaluate the following inductive generalisations:

1. It has been sunny every day for the last week therefore it will be sunny tomorrow.

2. Clinical trials funded by pharmaceutical companies are more likely to produce a positive result than independently funded trials. The results of independently funded trials are therefore more reliable.

3. James performed very well in the tournament, against strong competition, therefore James will win the Open.

4. Since 7/7 I have been too frightened to use the Tube.

Answers on page 370

Causal Generalisations

Causal generalisations are an important type of inductive argument, given the human interest in explaining, predicting and manipulating events.

Imagine a car stops because it runs out of fuel. Had the car *not* run out of fuel the car would *not* have stopped. So it was a *necessary* condition of the car's continuing to move that it had fuel. That its fuel ran out was, therefore, *sufficient* for its stopping.

These are not claims about the conditions *logically* necessary or sufficient for the car's stopping or continuing to move. They are claims about *empirically* necessary and sufficient conditions.

We did not form the belief that cars stop when they run out of fuel by noting a correlation between cars running out of fuel and stopping. But every time this happens it further confirms the theories that led to the internal combustion engine. Causal claims are always based on and/or supported by observed correlations.

Here are two causal generalisations:

Argument 4.10:

Premise one: Every time Jane has worn her red jumper to an exam she has passed

Conclusion: Jane's red jumper is the cause of her exam success.

Argument 4.11:

Premise one: A meta-analysis of a systematic review of 5 double-blinded, randomised controlled trials, involving a total of 15,000 people, showed drug D was efficacious in alleviating symptoms of condition C in 75% of cases

Conclusion: Drug D might alleviate the symptoms of condition C in patient P.

Let's use these arguments to construct a list of questions by which to evaluate causal generalisations.

Causation and Correlation

Argument 4.10 assumes a correlation between A and B is *conclusive* evidence for the claim A causes B. This is false.

Correlations might be:

- **accidental** (Jane's having passed every exam she has taken whilst wearing her red jumper might be a coincidence.)

- **explained by a common cause** (Jane wears her red jumper *and* passes her exams when, and in each case *because*, she is feeling confident.)

- **the result of a causal relation that runs the other way** (Jane's past exam successes might be the cause of her wearing her red jumper.)

A causal generalisation will be better for ruling out such possibilities. Let's consider argument 4.11 from this perspective.

> *Here is a clip from Freakonomics about correlation not implying causation:*
> *http://www.youtube.com/watch?v=IbODqslc4Tg*

Eliminating Correlation Without Causation

That the correlation between taking drug D and the alleviation of the symptoms of condition C suffers from none of the three defects mentioned is well-supported by the evidence cited by argument 4.11.

The correlation is not accidental.

People often complain about symptoms when they are at their worst. This means the symptoms might spontaneously get better whatever happens. This is called 'regression to the mean'.

A causes B *only* when it is the case that had A not occurred B would not have occurred. If a patient's symptoms improved spontaneously, therefore, the claim that drug D caused symptom-alleviation would be unjustified.

Argument 4.11, though, tells us that the five trials reviewed were 'controlled'. This means that patients were divided into two groups, the members of only one of which took drug D. Because groups were chosen at random, they had roughly the same chance of spontaneous symptom-alleviation.

The trials were controlled *and* 'double blinded'. So no-one, patient or doctor, knew who was taking drug D. Any 'placebo effect' would also, therefore, have been common to both groups.

Comparison of the two groups justifies us in saying that taking drug D *made the difference* in alleviating symptoms.

This paper claims, on the basis of its appearance in mouse models in addition to human beings, that the correlation between trisomy 21 and DS is not accidental, but causal: http://www.nature.com/scitable/topicp age/trisomy-21-causes- down-syndrome-318

There is no common cause

Imagine that in each trial group-allocation was performed by a lovesick young male doctor who unconsciously allocated to the experimental group only attractive young women.

We might then say that being an attractive young woman caused the taking of drug D (at least it explains it). Being found attractive might, furthermore, have alleviated C-symptoms.
Argument 4.11 tells us, though, that all the trials were *randomised*, i.e. people were allocated to groups *at random*. This protects against group-members having anything in common *other* than the intervention given (and the placebo effect and regression to the mean). It further justifies our claiming that it was drug D that made the difference.

The causal relation (if any) is from taking drug D to symptom alleviation

The 15,000 chosen for the trials were selected because they had C-symptoms. Their symptoms were alleviated, therefore, *after* the trial started.

To the extent that causes occur *before* their effects, this justifies our claiming that *if* there is a causal relation between taking drug D, and the alleviation of C-symptoms, it is the former that causes the latter not vice versa.

Systematic Reviews and Meta-Analyses

The objectivity of the causal claim in argument 4.11 is ensured by its being based on a 'meta-analysis' of a 'systematic review' of trials of drug D.

A 'systematic review' is conducted when the published results of *all* trials meeting certain conditions are reviewed. In this case trials might have been required to:

- be testing drug D's efficacy in alleviating C-symptoms;

- be large, double-blinded, randomised controlled trials.

A 'meta-analysis' is conducted when reviewers produce a summary of *all* the data yielded by the trials reviewed. It irons out distortions not ironed out by the trials themselves. If one trial suggests drug D is *not* efficacious, but four trials suggest it is, a summary of results might go either way depending on the size of each trial and the data collected.

A meta-analysis will help compensate for missing data (perhaps someone didn't complete the trial?) and incorrect data (perhaps someone lied?).

Each trial might have dealt differently with such problems. But when the trials are compared and contrasted by a meta-analysis, such differences will have less impact on the conclusions drawn.

> *The logo of the Cochrane Collaboration, which conducts meta- analyses of clinical trials, is a 'blobbogram', summarizing results from trials designed to determine whether steroids promote the survival of premature babies. It shows that steroids reduce the chances of a child dying by half. Many babies died for want of knowledge of this summary. Read the full story on pages 14-16 of Ben Goldacre's book Bad Pharma:. Here's is Goldacre's website: http://www.badscience.net/books/bad-pharma/ and learn more about the Cochrane Collaboration here: http://www.cochrane.org/*

Negative Data

Meta-analyses are based on collecting *all* the data published by trials meeting certain conditions. But imagine that 10 large doubly blinded randomised trials on the efficacy of drug D in alleviating C-symptoms had been conducted, yet none of the results were published because they were negative.

In such a situation even the results of the meta-analysis will be distorted.

In his book <u>Bad Pharma</u> (Fourth Estate, 2012 and available here: http://www.amazon.co.uk/Bad-Pharma-companiesmislead-patients/dp/0007350740)

Ben Goldacre claims it is common for pharmaceutical companies not to publish negative data.

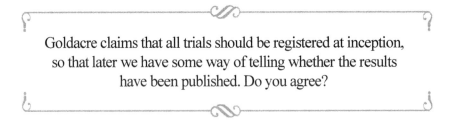

Goldacre claims that all trials should be registered at inception, so that later we have some way of telling whether the results have been published. Do you agree?

Causation and Determination

Argument 4.11 convincingly suggests that there is a causal relationship between taking drug D and the alleviation of C-symptoms. But this causal relationship does not appear to be deterministic. Symptoms were alleviated for only 75% of the patients taking drug D.

To justify claiming that a causal relation is deterministic we'd have to observe an *exceptionless* correlation between cause and effect.

158

Even then the PUN would ensure an exception might be imminent. Despite the fact that exceptionless correlations are so rare, many people still believe that causation is deterministic. Albert Einstein, for one, believed 'God doesn't play dice'.

Hidden Variables And Statistical Laws

Appeal to 'hidden variables' enables us to preserve the view that causation is deterministic in the face of observations of exceptions that might seem to falsify such talk. These arise whenever laws interact. So, striking a match will cause the match to light. But only if oxygen is present (the striking was hard enough, the match was dry…..).

But many scientists now reject the idea that *all* causation is deterministic. These scientists believe that there are causal laws that are probabilistic *by their very nature.*

So the causal relation identified by argument 4.11 might be an irreducibly statistical law of the form: 'Drug D alleviates symptoms of condition C in 75% of cases'.

The probabilistic form of this causal relation might also be explained by the presence of some unknown condition, S, such that drug D works *deterministically* to cure the symptoms of condition C, but only in those with condition S.

> *Here is the physicist Stephen Hawking on the subject of statistical laws:*
> *http://www.hawking.org.uk/does-god-play-dice.html*

Questions To Evaluate Causal Generalisations

Our comparison of arguments ten and eleven generates the following list of questions to ask of causal generalisations:

1. Are the premises true?

2. Was the evidence recorded objectively?

3. Are we arguing from a large enough sample?

4. Is the sample from which we are arguing from, or to, representative?

5. Might the correlations be accidental?

6. Might the correlations result from a common cause?

7. Might any causal relation run the other way?

8. Are exceptions to the correlation the result of hidden variables, or is the causal relation statistical?

Abductive Arguments

Abductive arguments go from claims that a given hypothesis is the best explanation of something, to the claim that the hypothesis is true.

Abductive arguments enable us to appeal to causes that are unobservable. Inductive and causal generalisations do not permit this, both being based on and confirmed by observations.

The traditional arguments for the existence of God rely on abduction. The existence of God is postulated, for example, as the best explanation for the existence of the universe.

Science also uses such arguments. The existence of gravity is postulated, for example, as the best explanation of things staying put on Earth instead of being spun off by the Earth's rotation.

Here are two abductive arguments:

Argument 4.12:

Premise One: The burglar was 1.84m or over

Premise Two: Smith is 1.90m and was seen loitering by the house the day it was burgled

Conclusion: The best explanation of the evidence is that Smith is the burglar.

Argument 4.13:

Premise One: When a star is receding a redshift is seen in the planet's characteristic spectrum

Premise two: The velocity of the recession of a star correlates with the amount of redshift

Conclusion   That star R is receding from us at velocity V is the best explanation of there being a redshift of amount A in the characteristic spectrum of star R.

Induction and Circularity

Both these arguments exhibit a sort of circularity. In argument 4.13, for example, the redshift in star R's characteristic spectrum is evidence *for* the hypothesis that Star R is receding from us, and evidence *confirming* this hypothesis (to some degree).

The same phenomenon is at work in inductive and causal generalisations (observations of black ravens provided us with evidence *for*, and evidence *confirming*, the hypothesis 'all ravens are black', and correlations between A and B are evidence *for*, and confirmation of, the hypothesis 'A causes B').

This circularity is not vicious. A circularity is benign (or 'virtuous') whenever it is logically possible both to accept the premises and deny the conclusion. Circularity is only vicious when it is not possible to accept the premise of a circular argument *and* deny the conclusion (because the conclusion *is* one of the premises).

The Best Explanation

If the candidate hypotheses from which an explanation is chosen as 'the best' is a set of not-very-good hypotheses, the hypothesis will only be the best of a bad lot. It is usually required, therefore, that an explanation be satisfactory in its own right before it can be 'the best'.

But what it is for an explanation to be 'satisfactory'? What it is for it to be *more satisfactory* than other explanations?

Attempts have been made to explain this in terms of the 'theoretical virtues', and 'contrastive questions'.

The Theoretical Virtues

The 'theoretical virtues' are characteristics such that the greater the degree to which an explanation has them the better that explanation is supposed to be. Here is a list of such characteristics:

- generality;

- comprehensiveness;

- precision;

- simplicity;

- the more information on underlying mechanisms the better;

- the more coherent with other accepted explanations the better.

But is God the more theoretically virtuous explanation for the origin of the universe, or is the Big Bang better? The latter is certainly more coherent with other accepted explanations. But some suggest that the Big Bang can't be explained without appeal to God. If this is right, the former is the more comprehensive explanation.

The theoretical virtues must be weighed against each other. This is not a simple matter, and there are no guiding rules.

Contrastive Questions

Contrastive questions mark the fact that it is never the case that there is a single cause for any phenomenon. There will *always* be many causes working together. Two questions are *contrastive* when they ask about contrasting aspects of a phenomenon.

If for example we are interested in the cause of Fred's lung cancer we might ask why Fred developed lung cancer *and Ruth didn't*. Or we might ask why Fred developed cancer *and Joan didn't*.

If Fred smokes and Ruth doesn't, we might postulate smoking as our explanation. But if both Fred and Joan smoke, that cannot be the answer.

The cause is that which makes the difference. When the *differences* are different, the causes might be different too.

The *best* explanation might be that which best answers a given question.

Questions To Ask Of Abductive Arguments:

1. Are the premises true?

2. Does the explanation display more theoretical virtues, or exemplify them better, than any other candidate explanation?

3. Is the explanation better than other candidate explanations *as an answer to the question being asked*?

Exercise 4.5: Evaluate the following abductive argument.

"God exists. This is a world of *values*, a world in which things *matter*, a world in which love exists and people do things because they *care* about others. Science can explain the evolutionary *origin* of values, but not the *nature* of values. For that we must appeal to God.

Answers on page 371

Arguments From Analogy

Arguments from analogy appeal to a similarity between two things to justify the claim that because one of them has given characteristic, the other will *also* have that characteristic.

Here are two arguments from analogy:

Argument 4.14:

Premise one   Jan first met Tom the night she was wearing a new dress from Bop Shop

Premise two: Tonight Sam is going to wear her new dress from Bop Shop

Conclusion: Tonight will be the night Sam meets the love of her life!

Argument 4.15:

Premise one: This essay is by Henry James, written after his US lecture series of 1904

Premise two: Fred enjoyed the last James essay, also written after the US tour

Conclusion: Fred would enjoy this essay.

Are you as confident that Sam will meet the love of her life tonight, as you are of Fred's chances of enjoying the unread essay? If not, why not?

To what extent are Sam's chances of meeting the love of her life enhanced by:

- her wearing her new Bop Shop dress;

- the fact Jan met Tom whilst wearing *her* new Bop Shop dress.

Relevance

Do we believe that *Jan's* dress was relevant to her meeting Tom? If not, it is legitimate to question the extrapolation we are being asked to make.

But perhaps Tom noticed the new dress and started a conversation? If so why did Tom notice the dress? Did Jan feel good in it and sparkle in a way that caught Tom's eye? Did she look so stylish that Tom was impressed, or so *terrible* that Tom teased her? Did it bring out the colour of her eyes?

How similar, furthermore, is *Sam's* new dress to Jan's? Is this relevant? How similar is *Sam* to *Jan*? Does Sam sparkle when wearing a new dress? Is she stylish? Is the love of Sam's life likely to notice a new dress, its stylishness or the sparkle of the girl wearing it?

The sheer number of questions to be asked about argument 4.14 reveals its weakness.

In argument 4.15 we are being asked to extrapolate from these facts:

- Henry James wrote this essay after his American tour;

- Fred has previously enjoyed essays written by James at this time.

We are being asked to extrapolate *to* the claim that Fred will enjoy another essay that James wrote after his American tour.

There will be differences between the unread essay and the earlier one. Perhaps they cover different topics, or the same topic from different angles. Perhaps they're published by different publishers? Perhaps one is hard-back, the other paperback?

But are these differences relevant? Probably not. The author and period in which he was writing, on the other hand, are strong predictors of the likelihood of enjoyment.

Questions To Ask Of Arguments From Analogy:

1. *from* which property (or properties) are we being asked to extrapolate?

2. *to* which property (or properties) are we being asked to extrapolate?

3. are the properties from which we are being asked to extrapolate *relevant* to the properties to which we are being asked to extrapolate?

4. are there are any significant differences to be taken into account (in what we are extrapolating from, or in what we are extrapolating to)?

Exercise 4.5: What do you think of this analogy?

In the Republic, book IV, Plato argued that a just state is analogous to a just individual. The latter, he argues, is just only when the three parts of his soul - reason, will and emotion - are properly ordered (so the will guides the emotions as reason directs). The former is just only when the three classes of people (philosopher-rulers, soldiers and people) are properly ordered (so the soldiers guide the people as directed by the rulers).

Answer on page 371

Arguments From Authority

Here are two arguments from authority:

Argument 4.16:

Premise one: Stephen Hawking says philosophy is dead

Premise two: Stephen Hawking is a famous physicist

Conclusion: Philosophy is dead.

Argument 4.17:

Premise one: Stephen Hawking says black holes emit radiation

Premise two: Stephen Hawking is a famous physicist

Conclusion: Black holes emit radiation.

It is a necessary condition for the success of an argument from authority that the authority *be* an authority, and that he is an authority in the appropriate field.

An Authority on *What?*

Stephen Hawking is a world-renowned physicist. He is not a philosopher. Argument 4.17 is therefore better than argument 4.16.

Controversy Amongst Authorities

It is not a sufficient condition of being right that one is an authority in the field. Authorities sometimes disagree. Hawking, for example, is a supporter of the 'Many-Worlds' interpretation of Quantum Physics. This is a widely, but not universally, accepted view: there are reputable physicists who reject it.

The fact that Hawking is a world-renowned physicist does not, therefore, ensure he is always right even about *physics* (which is not to say he *is* wrong, just that he is not certainly right)

Argument 4.17, however, offers a conclusion which is now uncontroversial. It is reasonable to assume that Hawking *is* right.

Fields in which *all* Authority is questionable

Physics is clearly a field in which talk of authority is apt. People don't become authorities in physics unless they have studied for many years, and proven their worth in the eyes of others who have studied just as long. But not all fields are like this.

Astrology, for example, is not obviously such a field. Although there would be many people who claim to be authorities in this field there would be just as many people who would argue there can be no authorities in a field in which there is no truth.

We needn't enter the debate about whether astrology is a genuine field of study. We need only recognise that its credentials are questioned by many. Recognising this, we should accept that where a *field* is not accepted as authoritative, there can be no genuine *authorities*.

Bias and Authority Citing

Sometimes we probably have to accept an argument from authority. When we know nothing of a topic, it is probably better to accept what the authorities say.

To the extent, though, that these authorities might have an axe to grind scepticism is justified. If a famous sportsperson is being paid to advertise the trainers of a certain manufacturer, it might be better to reserve judgement.

It might be better to reserve judgement also when someone who isn't an authority cites an authority. In such a situation we should ask for a reference so we can check out for ourselves what the authority says.

It is cause for suspicion if someone quoting an authority is unable to provide a reference that would enable us to check for ourselves.

Is It Plausible?

Whilst Prime Minister, Margaret Thatcher remarked 'there is no such thing as society'. As a politician, Thatcher might reasonably be thought as an authority in this area. Does this justify us in thinking her remark is true?

Many would say 'no' because Thatcher's remark is obviously implausible (and she had an axe to grind). Even when an authority pronounces in their area of authority, an obvious implausibility should be taken seriously.

But the claim 'the Earth is spherical' (or 'ellipsoidal' or whichever word you prefer so long as it is not 'flat'!) must once have seemed hugely implausible. Implausibility does not entail falsehood. Some have claimed that, read in its context and understood properly, Mrs Thatcher's remark is actually true.

The Principle of Charity exhorts us always to reflect on the possibility that we are wrong to dismiss something as implausible. This is true even if the person claiming it is someone whose views many love to hate!

Exercise 4.7: Is the following an argument from analogy or authority? Is it a strong argument?

"Philosophy of Science is as much use to scientists as ornithology is to birds." (Richard Feynmann)

Answers on page 372

Questions To Ask Of Arguments From Authority:

1. is the 'authority' truly authoritative?

2. is this authority authoritative in the right area?

3. do authorities in this field agree?

4. Is this a field that generates genuine authorities?

5. could this authority be biased?

6. is what this authority says plausible?

7. is there a reference I can check?

Summary

At the beginning of this chapter you were told that after a careful reading of it you would be able to:

- explain why induction relies on the PUN;

- show that the PUN cannot be justified;

- argue for the claim that induction is non-rational;

- explain the paradoxes of confirmation;

- explain why auxiliary assumptions are required;

- understand why Popper argued that scientists never use induction;

- evaluate Popper's argument;

- explain the arguments for and against the idea that induction is inferior to deduction;

- enumerate the different types of inductive argument;

- list the questions needed to evaluate each kind of inductive argument.

Can you do these things? If not, go back and re-read the relevant sections.

Otherwise the time has come to move onto chapter five. Well done, you are over half way through this book!

CHAPTER FIVE

Evaluating Deductive Arguments

This chapter corresponds to the *fourth* podcast in my series: **Critical Reasoning: A Romp Through The Foothills of Logic.** The video podcast can be found at metafore.com/ CR5video, the audio-only podcast at metafore.com/ CR5audio, slides at metafore.com/CR5slides, and a transcript at http://mariannetalbot.co.uk/transcripts/.

Podcast Warning: I have reversed the order in which I discuss induction and deduction. This chapter really does correspond to the fourth podcast, rather than the fifth.

We saw in chapter four that there is no systematic method for evaluating inductive arguments. There is such a method for evaluating deduction. By the end of this chapter you will know what this method is.

In chapter three we saw that a deductive argument is good iff it is valid. It is valid iff there is no logically possible situation in which all its premises are true and its conclusion false. It is important, as you saw in chapter three, that validity is defined in terms of *logical* rather than *empirical* possibility.

This definition of validity has implications that may seem strange at first. It also has implications that *are* strange. In this chapter we shall draw out these implications, dispelling the strangeness of the first set, and noting those of the second set. We shall reflect on the relation between validity and truth, and validity and persuasiveness.

Finally we'll learn the method by which *any* deductive argument can (in principle) be tested. This involves setting out the argument logic-book style, creating a 'counterexample set', and testing this counterexample set for consistency.

Don't worry if this seems unintelligible. It will be clear by the end of this chapter, a careful reading of which will ensure you will be able to:

- understand and explain the implications of the definition of validity

- explain what it is for an argument to preserve, but not to generate, truth;

- explain the procedure for testing deductive arguments;

- understand why this procedure works;

- create counterexample sets for deductive arguments;

- recognise when a counterexample set is consistent or inconsistent;

- explain the implications of the consistency or inconsistency of a counterexample set for the validity of an argument;

- explain why counterexample sets are not arguments;

- recognise arguments that are valid but unpersuasive.

As usual, at the end of the chapter, you'll check all this before you move on to the next chapter.

The Definition of Validity

The definition of validity tells us:

(i) it is a *sufficient* condition of an argument's being valid that there is no logically possible situation in which all its premises are true and its conclusion false (i.e. if there is no such situation the argument is valid);

(ii) it is a *necessary* condition of an argument's being valid that there is no logically possible situation in which all its premises are true and its conclusion false (i.e. is *only* if there is no such situation that the argument is valid).

This has some counter-intuitive consequences. In particular, undergraduates often have trouble wrapping their minds around the first two of the following three facts:

1. arguments with false premises and a false conclusion can be valid;

2. arguments with false premises and a true conclusion can be valid;

3. arguments with true premises and a true conclusion can be valid.

But these *are* facts. They follow from the definition of validity. According to that definition the only arguments that *cannot* be valid are those with true premises and a false conclusion.

To demonstrate that arguments of the first three types can be valid or invalid let's look at a valid and an invalid argument of each:

Situation one: false premises and a false conclusion

Argument 5.1: valid

Premise one: All fish have wings

Premise two: Whales are fish

Conclusion: Whales have wings.

Argument 5.2: invalid

Premise one: All fish have scales

Premise two: Whales have scales

Conclusion: Whales are fish.

The premises of arguments 5.1 and 5.2, and the conclusions, are all false. Argument 5.1 is valid. Argument 5.2 is not.

To see that argument 5.1 is valid, consider the fact that *if* (this is a very important 'if') the premises were true, the conclusion *would have to be* true (this is a very important 'would have to be'). The conclusion *couldn't* be false, *if* the premises *were* all true. That the premises aren't *in fact* true is irrelevant.

In claiming that the conclusion *would have to be* true if the premises were true, and that the conclusion *couldn't* be false if the premises were true, I am appealing to the laws of logic (as we currently understand them). It is logic *itself* that ensures the impossibility of a situation in which the premises of a valid argument are true and yet its conclusion false.

A logical contradiction would be generated, wouldn't it, in supposing that the premises of argument 5.1 were true and yet its conclusion false? This ensures the validity of the argument.

178

So despite the fact that every single sentence in argument 5.1 is false the argument is *still* valid.

But argument 5.2 is not valid. Its premises would be true and its conclusion false if whales have scales but are *not* fish. The very existence of this logically possible situation, one in which the premises are true yet the conclusion false, ensures that the argument is invalid.

Note carefully that the first premise of argument 5.2 does not say 'all *and only* fish have scales'. If it did say this then the argument *would* be valid.

It is not possible to tell, from the fact that the premises and the conclusion of an argument are all *actually* false, whether or not the argument is valid. We can determine this *only* by answering the question: is it logically possible for all the premises to be true and yet the conclusion false?

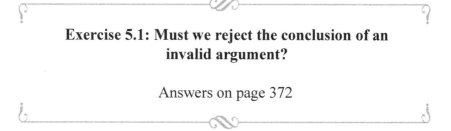

Exercise 5.1: Must we reject the conclusion of an invalid argument?

Answers on page 372

Situation two: premises all false, conclusion true

Argument 5.3: valid

Premise one: All fish have lungs

Premise two: Whales are fish

Conclusion: Whales have lungs.

Argument 5.4: invalid

Premise one: All fish have scales

Premise two: Whales have scales

Conclusion: Whales are not fish.

The premises of arguments 5.3 and 5.4 are all false. The conclusions, though, are true. Argument 5.3 is valid. Argument 5.4 is not.

To see that argument 5.3 is valid, consider again the fact that *if* (that important 'if' again) the premises *were* true the conclusion *would have to be* true (again that important 'would have to be'). Again the conclusion *couldn't* be false if the premises were all true.

Again it is logic that tells us this. A logical contradiction would again be generated in supposing that the premises of argument 5.3 were true and yet its conclusion false. This ensures that the argument is valid.

Argument 5.4, though, is not valid. There is a logically possible situation in which all its premises are true, and yet its conclusion is false; that in which non-fish have scales. Being a fish is a *sufficient* condition for having scales, on premise one, but not a *necessary* one.

Again, therefore, it is not possible to tell simply from the fact that the premises of an argument are all *actually* false and its conclusion *actually* true, whether or not the argument is valid. As before we can determine this *only* by deciding whether or not there is a logically possible situation in which all the premises are true yet the conclusion false.

Situation three: true premises and true conclusion

Argument 5.5: valid

Premise one: All cats meow

Premise two: The Queen's corgi does not meow

Conclusion: The Queen's corgi is not a cat.

Argument 5.6: invalid

Premise one: All cats meow

Premise two: The Queen's corgi is not a cat

Conclusion: The Queen's corgi doesn't meow.

The premises of these arguments are all true, and their conclusions are also true. That it is not this fact that makes argument 5.5 valid is obvious from the fact that argument 5.6 is *not* valid.

Argument 5.5 is valid for the same reason that arguments 5.1 and 5.3 are valid: there is no logically possible situation in which its premises are all true and its conclusion false.

Argument 5.6 is *invalid* for the same reason that arguments 5.2 and 5.4 were invalid: there *is* a logically possible situation in which its premises are all true and its conclusion false. This is the situation in which the Queen's corgi *does* meow. This may be an *empirically* impossible situation, but it is not *logically* impossible. It is only logical impossibility that matters.

Truth and Validity

People sometimes find it hard to accept there can be valid arguments the premises of which, and indeed the conclusions of which, can be false. I think this is because they confuse truth and validity. Perhaps they think that as truth is good and validity is good, truth and validity must coincide.

This is a *very* bad inference. It is actually the fallacy of 'Undistributed Middle'. You can read about it here: http://www.fallacyfiles.org/undismid.html

Validity and truth are related. But they are not the same thing. Validity is truth-*preserving;* if the premises of a valid argument are true the conclusion of that argument *must,* as a matter of logic, be true. Validity is *not* truth-*generating*; if the premises of a valid argument are false, then the conclusion might be either true *or* false.

We learn *nothing* about the truth of a conclusion from a valid argument the premises of which are false.

Exercise 5.2: If the conclusion of a valid argument can be false, why is validity so useful?

Answers on page 373

Bivalence Again

The moral of the last few sections is that validity is a relation between the *possible* truth values of the premises and the conclusion of an argument claim. The only time the *actual* truth values of an argument tell us anything about its validity is when the premises are actually true, and the conclusion actually false. In such a situation we know that the argument is *not* valid. Any other combination of *actual* truth values is irrelevant in that the argument might be either valid or invalid.

Luckily we know, because we have accepted bivalence, that all sentences have one of only two possible truth values: they are either true or they are false. There is no third truth value, and there are no truth value gaps. This makes it easy for us 'mechanically' to test an argument for validity. We'll learn how to do this in chapter seven.

For now it is important only to see that the claim made by *anyone* who uses an argument (rather than simply mentioning it) is that his conclusion follows from his premises. If the argument he is using is deductive this amounts to the claim that there is no logically possible situation in which all his premises are true and his conclusion false.

When we are evaluating a deductive argument it is *this* claim that we must test.

Testing Argument Claims

We saw in chapter three (page 86) that there are two questions that must be asked to evaluate any argument:

1. are the premises true?

2. does the conclusion follow?

It is only the second of these questions that concerns us here. It is also only *deductive* arguments that concern us here. Deductive 'following from' is quite different from inductive 'following from'.

If we are asking, of a deductive argument whether its conclusion follows from its premises, what we are asking is: *is there a logically possible situation in which all the premises of this argument could be true and yet its conclusion false?*

If the answer is 'yes' then the argument claim (the claim that the argument is valid) is false (because the argument is invalid). If the answer is 'no' then the argument claim is true (and the argument is valid).

The Strength of Deduction

If you do not accept the premises of a deductive argument, the argument claim is of no interest to you. You'll be interested only in arguing about the truth of the premises.

But if you *do* accept the premises of a deductive argument, or even if you simply think they *might* be true, then the argument claim becomes important.

If the person using the argument is right to claim that it is logically impossible for his premises to be true and his conclusion false then:

(a) if you *accept* the premises you will *have* to accept the conclusion, it would be a failure of reason to reject it;

(b) if you accept the premises *might* be true, then you are logically *obliged* to accept that the conclusion might be true too.

This is the strength of deduction.

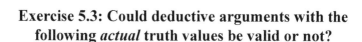

Exercise 5.3: Could deductive arguments with the following *actual* truth values be valid or not?

1. Premises all true, and conclusion true?

2. Some premises true, some premises false, conclusion true?

3. Premises all true, conclusion not true?

4. Premises all false, conclusion false?

5. Premises all false, conclusion true?

Answers on page 373

Strange Implications

Arguments can be valid even if their premises, *and* their conclusions, are false. But there is another strange implication of the definition of validity. This time the strangeness is not one we can entirely dispel.

It is that arguments can be valid, and even sound, *without* being persuasive.

At the beginning of chapter three (page 86) I said soundness was a *necessary* but not a *sufficient* condition of being able to acquire knowledge from the argument. Unpersuasive arguments are those that are valid and/or sound, but not such that we can acquire knowledge from them.

Unfortunately they can be used in such a way that we *think* we are acquiring knowledge from them.

Circular arguments, and arguments that are valid by virtue of *the paradoxes of entailment*, are both arguments of this type. Let's look at each:

Circular Arguments

Argument 5.7:

Premise one: All whales are mammals

Conclusion: All whales are mammals.

This argument is valid, and it is sound. The conclusion of argument 5.7 *is* the premise of argument 5.7. As the premise is true, therefore, the conclusion *must* be true.

How could there be a logically possible situation in which premise one of argument 5.7 is true, yet its conclusion false? All circular arguments, like argument 5.7, are valid.

But no-one should be persuaded of anything by circular arguments. Anyone who believes the premise, after all, believes the conclusion. But they do not believe the conclusion *as a result of the argument.*

Circular arguments cannot *persuade* us of anything.

You might say 'but who would be persuaded by this argument? It is obviously useless'.

Unfortunately, circularity is easily obscured. Validity, you will remember, is monotonic, it cannot be changed by the addition of further information.

Argument 5.7 is obviously circular, but is argument 5.8?

Argument 5.8:

Premise one: Mammals have live young

Premise two: Fish do not have live young

Premise three: Whales have live young

Premise four: All whales are mammals

Premise five: No whale is a fish

Premise six: No mammals are fish

Conclusion: All whales are mammals.

The circularity of argument 5.7 is not obvious. Nevertheless, argument 5.8 is merely argument 5.7 with some extra premises. The monotonicity of validity ensures, therefore, that argument 5.8 is valid too. But its circularity is not obvious.

Human beings, as natural validity-detectors, will often detect the validity of a circular argument, but not the explanation of its validity. They may take themselves to have been persuaded by an argument like argument 5.8 that all whales are mammals. But they are not being *persuaded* of anything. They are simply having their original beliefs fed back to them.

The Paradoxes of Entailment

Here is another pair of arguments both of which are valid, neither of which is persuasive:

Argument 5.9:

Premise one: Grass is green

Conclusion: 2+2=4.

Argument 5.10:

Premise one: $2 + 2 = 5$

Conclusion: Grass is green.

It is hugely counter-intuitive, but arguments 5.9 and 5.10 are both valid arguments. This is because:

- the conclusion of argument 5.9 is a tautology (a statement such that there is no logically possible situation in which it is false);

- the premise of argument 5.10 is a contradiction (a statement such that there is no logically possible situation in which it is true).

Exercise 5.4: I have just told you why arguments nine and ten are valid, but can you say more?

Answers on page 374

The paradoxes of entailment might seem inexplicable. In fact they fall out of the fact that the *content* of an argument is irrelevant to its validity or invalidity. All that matters is the structure of the argument and the possible truth values of its constituent sentences. Consider the fact, also, that strange things fall out of other definitions. It would be much better, wouldn't it, to have a definition of 'fish' and 'mammal' on which whales are fish rather than mammals. But the universe didn't oblige.

Nevertheless our definition of validity has underpinned computer science: it may throw up some oddities, but it works.

Note again how easy it would be to obscure the fact that two premises contradict each other. Careful choice of wording might also obscure the fact that a conclusion is tautological. Such arguments might *seem* persuasive. They might even persuade. But they shouldn't because they are *not* persuasive.

Testing Deductive Arguments for Validity

We can now learn how to evaluate deductive arguments. Claims to the effect that an argument is valid can be tested by means of the notion of *consistency.*

Here again, from chapter 3 page 93, are the definitions of 'consistency' and 'inconsistency'

Def: **a set of sentences is *consistent* iff there is a logically possible situation in which all the sentences in the set can be true together.**

Def: **a set of sentences is *inconsistent* iff there is no logically possible situation in which all the sentences in the set can be true together.**

To decide whether an argument is valid we need to decide whether there is a logically possible situation in which its premises are true and its conclusion false.

This we can decide by taking the *counterexample set* of the argument, and testing it for consistency.

The counterexample set of an argument is that set consisting of all the premises of the argument, plus *the negation* of its conclusion, i.e. the conclusion plus 'it is not the case that' tacked in front. The negation of the conclusion is the contradiction of the conclusion. If the conclusion is true, the negation of the conclusion will be false, and vice versa.

If *there is* a logically possible situation in which the counterexample set of an argument is *consistent* the argument will be *invalid.*

After all, if:

- there is a logically possible situation in which *all the premises and the negation of the conclusion* are true;

and

- the negation of the conclusion is the contradictory of the conclusion, so if it is true, the conclusion is *false* and vice versa;

then this very situation shows that the argument claim is *false*: that there is a logically possible situation in which all the premises of the argument are true *yet* the conclusion false.

But if the counterexample set is *inconsistent* the argument will be *valid*. After all if:

- there is *no* logically possible situation in which *all the premises and the negation of the conclusion* are true together;

and

- the negation of the conclusion is the contradictory of the conclusion, so if it is true, the conclusion is *false* and vice versa;

then there is no logically possible situation in which all the premises are true and the conclusion false. The argument claim is true.

In creating the counterexample set we are, in effect, pretending the conclusion is false, and seeing if we can find a logically possible situation where this supposedly false conclusion is true at the same time as all the premises are true.

Here is an example just to make sure of this important point. Take the following argument:

Premise one: If it is Friday then Marianne is wearing jeans

Premise two: It is Friday

Conclusion: Marianne is wearing jeans.

First we list the two premises:

If it is Friday then Marianne is wearing jeans

It is Friday

Then we negate the conclusion:

It is not the case Marianne is wearing jeans.

Then we put them together:

If it is Friday then Marianne is wearing jeans

It is Friday

It is not the case that Marianne is wearing jeans.

Are the sentences in this set consistent? In other words, can they all be true together? I think it is easy to see that they are not. This means that there is *no* logically possible situation in which all the premises *and the negation of the conclusion* are true together.

This means that there is no situation in which all the premises are true, and the conclusion (the conclusion itself, not its negation) is false. The argument, therefore, is valid.

The Method

The systematic method by which to determine, of any deductive argument whether it is valid or invalid has four steps:

1. analyse the argument (set it out logic-book style);

2. create its 'counterexample set';

3. decide whether the counterexample set is consistent;

4. decide whether the argument is valid or invalid.

The method you are learning here cannot officially be applied to inductive arguments. In fact you *can* apply something similar to inductive arguments to test their strength. You will not, though, get the precision you can get when using it to test deductive arguments.

In the rest of this chapter we shall apply this method to a deductive argument for the claim, of an *inductive* argument, that it is valid. (You might have to read the previous sentence a couple of times – we are going to test an argument *about an argument*!) This will enable you simultaneously to:

*   familiarise yourself with the four step method;

*   consolidate your understanding of the difference between logical and empirical possibility.

Here is the inductive argument that will be said to be valid:

Argument 5.11:

Premise one: Thousands of babies born with trisomy 21 (henceforth T21) have Down's Syndrome (henceforth DS) and no baby born with T21 does not have DS

Conclusion: The next baby born with T21 will therefore have DS.

This argument is inductively strong. Indeed there might even be a law of nature ensuring that T21 empirically necessitates DS. But the premise of argument 5.11 does not *logically* necessitate its conclusion. Argument 5.11 is not, therefore, valid.

But we knew this. Inductive arguments are *never* valid. There is always a *logically* possible situation in which their premises are true and their conclusion false. So far as *logic* is concerned a child might be born tomorrow with T21 but *not DS*.

It is *hugely* important to remember that *empirical* necessity is different from *logical* necessity, the latter being the requirement for the validity of a deductive argument. If you'd like to remind yourself of the difference between empirical and logical necessity refer back to chapter 3 pages 92-102

An Imaginary Interlocutor

We can imagine, though, an interlocutor who argues:

"Hang on, if it really is the case that thousands of babies born with T21 have DS and no baby born with T21 does not have DS then it is *impossible* that a baby should be born with T21 but not DS. After all", *our imaginary interlocutor will continue*, "if every baby with T21 also has DS then there is clearly a causal law relating T21 and DS. If there is a causal law relating T21 and DS, however, then T21 *necessitates* DS. But if T21 necessitates DS, then the birth of a baby with T21 and not DS *is impossible*. This means that if the premise of argument 5.11 is true, the conclusion *must be true*, and argument 5.11 is *valid*."

Please make a note of this argument because we shall be working on it below. You will certainly need a notebook and a pencil for working on this argument - it will seem hugely complicated, but so long as you keep the different steps that you are taking in mind you will - I promise - be able to make sense of it.

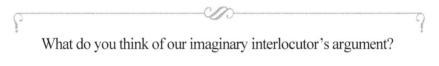

What do you think of our imaginary interlocutor's argument?

I hope you can see that our imaginary interlocutor hasn't understood that validity turns on *logical* not *empirical* impossibility.

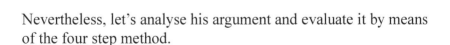

Nevertheless, let's analyse his argument and evaluate it by means of the four step method.

195

Step One: Analysing Our Imaginary Interlocutor's Argument

Our first step involves setting out our imaginary interlocutor's argument logic-book style.

Try analysing our imaginary interlocutor's argument for yourself, using the method of chapter two, before checking your analysis against mine.

Here are the steps to analysing an argument that we learned in chapter two:

1. identify the conclusion of the argument;

2. identify the premises of the argument;

3. remove cross references (if there are any);

4. eliminate any irrelevancies (if there are any);

5. remove inconsistent terminology (if there is any);

6. explicate malign suppressed premises (if there are any).

Warning: there are *two* arguments intertwined in our imaginary interlocutor's claims. I am going to analyse this argument by setting out logic-book style these two arguments and I suggest you do the same.

Here is *my* analysis of our imaginary interlocutor's argument. As you will see I have analysed it as *two* arguments.

Argument 5.12:

Premise one: If thousands of babies born with T21 have DS and no baby born with T21 does not have DS, then there is a causal law relating T21 and DS

Premise two: If there is a causal law relating T21 and DS then T21 necessitates DS

Premise three: If T21 *necessitates* DS then it is not possible that a baby should be born with T21 but *not* DS

Conclusion: If thousands of babies born with T21 have DS and no baby born with T21 does not have DS, then it is not possible that a baby should be born with T21 but *not* DS.

Argument 5.13:

Premise one: If the premises of argument 5.11 are true, then the conclusion *must* be true

Premise two: If an argument is such that if its premises are true its conclusion *must* be true, then the argument is *valid*

Conclusion: Argument 5.11 is valid.

By means of arguments 5.12 and 5.13 our imaginary interlocutor hopes to show that argument 5.11 is valid. You will want to make a note of both these arguments because we shall be discussing them again below.

I hope you can see both why our imaginary interlocutor *thinks* that arguments 5.12 and 5.13 enable him to achieve his aim, and why his confusing logical and empirical possibility undermines his belief he *has* achieved his aim.

But let's see whether or not arguments 5.12 and 5.13 are valid. As we have already performed the first step of our four step process (the analysis of our imaginary interlocutor's argument), we only have three steps to go. But each step must be applied to both arguments.

We'll start by applying our method to argument 5.12.

Step Two: Creating a Counterexample Set for Argument 5.12

Here is the definition of 'counterexample set':

> **Def:** the *'counterexample set'* of an argument is the set of sentences that consists in the premises of the argument plus *the negation of the conclusion of the argument.*

The counterexample set of argument 5.12, therefore, is the set of sentences consisting of each of the premises of argument 5.12 plus the sentence that is *the negation* of the conclusion of argument 5.12.

Negation

Here is the definition of 'negation':

> **Def:** the *negation* of a sentence is created by tacking 'it is not the case that' on to the front of the sentence.

The negation of a sentence logically contradicts that sentence. It, and the sentence, cannot both be true together. Nor can they be false together. To accept one is to be rationally obliged to reject the other and vice versa.

Exercise 5.5: Please provide counterexample sets for these deductive arguments.

Do not evaluate them for now (we'll do that later):

One

P1: If Lee is a Chinese Spy then Lee speaks Chinese

P2: Lee speaks Chinese

C: Lee is a Chinese Spy.

Two

P1: If Gemma was in the taxi last night then Gemma stole my purse

P2: Gemma was in the taxi last night

C: Gemma stole my purse.

Three:

P1: Peter is an accountant or James is an accountant

P2: Peter is not an accountant

C: James is an accountant.

Answers on page 375

To produce the counterexample set of argument 5.12, therefore, we need to negate its conclusion, by tacking 'it is not the case that' in front of it, and then we need to add the negated conclusion to the list of its premises.

Can you produce the counterexample set of argument 5.12?

Here is the counterexample set of argument 5.12:

Counterexample set of argument 5.12:

> If thousands of babies born with T21have DS and no baby born with T21 does not have DS, then there is a causal law relating T21 and DS.
>
> If there is a causal law relating T21 and DS then T21 *necessitates* DS.
>
> If T21 *necessitates* DS then it is not possible that a baby should be born with T21 but *not* DS.
>
> It is not the case that if thousands of babies born with T21 have DS and no baby born with T21 does not have DS, then it is not possible that a baby should be born with T21 but *not* DS.

You will want to make a note of this counterexample set because we shall be working on it below.

Please note there is no reference to premises and conclusion in this counterexample set. This is because the counterexample set is *not* an argument. It is just a set of sentences. No-one is asserting the negation of the conclusion, and the negation of the conclusion is not grounded on the other sentences of the set. So this set of sentences does not satisfy the conditions necessary for being an argument.

Having produced the counterexample set of argument 5.12 we can proceed to step three of our methodology – checking the counterexample set for consistency (again with respect to argument 5.12).

Step Three: Checking the Counterexample Set For Consistency

Our next task is to check whether the counterexample set we created in the last section is consistent. Here again are the definitions of 'consistent' and 'inconsistent':

> **Def:** a set of sentences is *consistent* iff it is logically possible for the sentences all to be true together.

> **Def:** a set of sentences is *inconsistent* iff it is not logically possible for them all to be true together.

We need to know, therefore, whether there is a logically possible situation in which all the sentences of the counterexample set for argument 5.12 are true together.

Do you think the counterexample set of argument 5.12 is consistent?

It is difficult to tell whether there is a logically possible situation in which all the sentences of the counterexample set for argument 5.12 can be true together, isn't it?

We can make life easier for ourselves by stripping this counterexample set of its content. It might be easier to tell, looking at the bare structure of this set of sentences, whether or not they are consistent.

Exercise 5.6: Providing an interpretation please strip the content from the counterexample set of argument 5.12.

See pages 116 - 117 for providing an interpretation.

Answers on page 376

Now we have stripped the counterexample set of its content, it is, I hope, much easier to see whether the counterexample set is consistent:

Counterexample set of argument 5.12 (form only):

If P then Q.

If Q then R.

If R then S.

It is not the case that if P then S.

It seems obvious (I hope), even without using the interpretation, that there is no logically possible situation in which the sentences of the counterexample set of argument 5.12 are all true together. The sentences are *inconsistent*.

Exercise 5.7: Providing an interpretation (see chapter three, page 116), please strip the counterexample sets below of their content, then decide whether they are consistent or not:

Counterexample set

One

If Lee is a Chinese spy then Lee speaks Chinese.

Lee speaks Chinese.

It is not the case that Lee is a Chinese spy.

Two

If Gemma was in the taxi last night then Gemma stole my purse.

Gemma was in the taxi last night.

It is not the case that Gemma stole my purse.

Three

Peter is an accountant or James is an accountant.

Peter is not an accountant.

It is not the case that James is an accountant.

Answers on page 377

We are now ready for our final move, with respect to argument 5.12.

Step Four: Deciding Whether Argument 5.12 Is Valid Or Invalid

The last step is easy so long as you remember something that seems highly counterintuitive, namely:

- if the counterexample set is *consistent* then the argument is *invalid.*

- if the counterexample set is *inconsistent* then the argument is *valid.*

This may seem counterintuitive. In my experience beginners in logic often think that because consistency is a good thing and validity is a good thing, *consistency* should go with validity and *inconsistency* should go with invalidity. This is analogous to the reasoning, discussed earlier, that results in the – false - belief that the premises of valid arguments can't be false. This is another example, in other words, of the fallacy of undistributed middle.

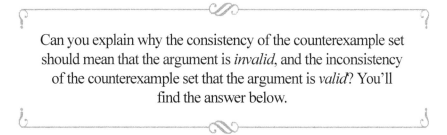

Can you explain why the consistency of the counterexample set should mean that the argument is *invalid*, and the inconsistency of the counterexample set that the argument is *valid*? You'll find the answer below.

The definition of validity tells us that an argument is valid iff there is no logically possible situation in which all its premises are true and its conclusion false. This means that:

- if an argument is valid, it will be logically impossible for the counterexample set to be consistent.

- if an argument is invalid, there must be a logically possible situation in which the sentences of the counterexample set are true together; so the set must be *consistent*.

Given that the counterexample set of argument 5.12 is *inconsistent*, therefore, then we know – with absolute certainty – that this argument is valid. Given the monotonicity of validity, furthermore, we know it is *conclusively* valid.

Exercise 5.8: Please decide, with respect to each of the arguments above, whether it is valid. If it is not valid please provide a counterexample.

Answers on page 378

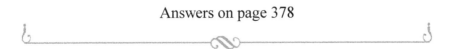

The claim that there is no logically possible situation in which the premises of this argument are true, and its conclusion false, is correct. Our imaginary interlocutor is *correct* to claim that this part of his argument, at least, is valid.

The Truth of the Conclusion of Argument 5.12

So, argument 5.12 is valid. We therefore know that *if* its premises are true, its conclusion *must* be true.

This doesn't tell us, of course, that the conclusion *is* true. All we know is that *if* the premises are true the conclusion *must* be true.

Exercise 5.9: Do you think that the premises of argument 5.12 are true?

Here are those premises again:

Premise one: If thousands of babies born with T21 have DS and no baby born with T21 does not have DS, then there is a causal law relating T21 and DS

Premise two: If there is a causal law relating T21 and DS then T21 necessitates DS

Premise three: If T21 *necessitates* DS then it is not possible that a baby should be born with T21 but *not* DS.

Answer on page 379

Argument 5.13

So we know that the first part of our imaginary interlocutor's argument is valid. But we haven't yet finished evaluating his argument. That argument fell into two parts. We have yet to evaluate the second part, argument 5.13.

Here it is:

Argument 5.13:

Premise one: If the premises of argument 5.11 are true, then the conclusion of argument 5.11 *must* be true

Premise two: If an argument is such that if its premises are true its conclusion *must* be true, then the argument is *valid*

Conclusion: Argument 5.11 is valid.

We *know* that the conclusion of argument 5.13 is false. If we were to find that this argument is valid, therefore, we know something for *certain*.

Exercise 5.10: Can you say what it is that we would know *for certain* on the basis of *knowing* that the conclusion of argument 5.13 is false, and *discovering* that argument 5.13 is valid?

Answer on page 379

Validity can usefully tell us when a conclusion *must* be true. It can also usefully tell us when a premise *must* be false.

So let's go through each of the three steps left of the four step method to decide whether argument 5.13 is valid or not.

Step Two: Creating the Counterexample Set for Argument 5.13

You are now familiar with the process of creating the counterexample set: all we do is produce a list of the premises, and then add to that list the negation of the conclusion. Here, then is the counterexample set of argument 5.13:

Counterexample set of argument 5.13:

> If the premises of argument 5.11 are true, then the conclusion of argument 5.11 must be true.
>
> If an argument is such that if its premises are true its conclusion *must* be true, then the argument is *valid*.
>
> It is not the case that argument 5.11 is valid.

Please note again that we have lost the labels 'premise' and 'conclusion'. The counterexample set is *not* an argument. No one is using it to try to convince anyone of anything. It is simply a set of sentences.

We now have the counterexample set and can proceed to steps three and four. Please make a note of this counterexample set because we'll be working on it below.

Steps Three and Four for Argument 5.13

When we started to test the counterexample set of argument 5.12 for consistency we saw that it was quite complicated. We dealt with this by stripping the counterexample set of its content. It was much easier, once we had only the form of the counterexample set, to see that it was inconsistent.

It is tempting, therefore, to strip the counterexample set of argument 5.13 of its content. Sadly, though, this is impossible. In chapter six we shall be learning the rudiments of formalisation. This will involve learning what *cannot* be formalised. We shall see there why argument 5.13 can't be formalised.

Luckily though, the counterexample set of argument 5.13 isn't nearly as complicated as that for argument 5.12. Looking at the English meanings should suffice.

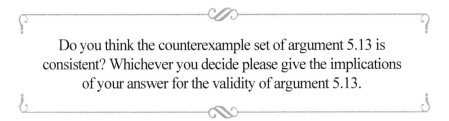

Do you think the counterexample set of argument 5.13 is consistent? Whichever you decide please give the implications of your answer for the validity of argument 5.13.

Have you have decided that the counterexample set of argument 5.13 is inconsistent and that, therefore, the argument is valid? If so, then given we know the *conclusion* of argument 5.13 is false, we also know that one of the *premises* of argument 5.13 must be false.

In fact the situation with argument 5.13 is much more complicated than it simply being the case that one of its premises is false.

Ambiguity Again

The word 'must' is ambiguous. It implies necessity and, as we have already seen, there are different types of necessity; *logical* and *empirical*. Thus we could be talking about a logical 'must' or an empirical 'must'. The fact that 'must' is ambiguous means that there are three possible situations with respect to argument 5.13:

1.   the 'must's of premises one and two are both *empirical*;

2.   the 'must's of premises one and two are both *logical*;

3.   the 'must's of premises one and two differ in meaning.

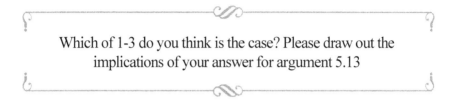

Which of 1-3 do you think is the case? Please draw out the
implications of your answer for argument 5.13

Situation one:

If the 'must's of premises one and two are both empirical then
premise two is false. It is *not* a sufficient condition of an
argument's being valid that if its premises are true its conclusion
must *empirically* be true. The only 'must' that would make
premise two true is a *logical* must.

Situation two:

If the 'must's of premises one and two are both logical, then
premise *one* is false. We know that there *is* a logically possible
situation in which the premises of argument 5.11 are both true and
yet its conclusion false. So far as logic is concerned it is entirely
possible that a baby might be born withT21 and yet not DS. There
are four situations in which this could happen:

1.   there is a causal law relating T21 and DS but it is
     statistical (the probability is *extremely high,* which is why
     no baby has yet been seen with T21 and not DS);

2. there is a causal law relating T21 and DS and it is deterministic, but there is a hidden variable (this variable, condition S is *extremely* common which is why we haven't yet seen a baby born with T21 and not DS because the baby lacks condition S);

3. there is no causal law relating T21 and DS, it is just a HUGE coincidence that no baby with T21 and not DS has yet been seen;

4. there is a deterministic causal law relating T21 and DS but it only operates in this world; in other possible worlds the laws of nature are different.

Situation three:

If the 'must's of premises one and two differ in meaning, then argument 5.13 is an *equivocation*. The *appearance* of validity turns on the fact that the word 'must' is being used with two different meanings.

In chapter eight we will be discussing fallacies and we will discuss equivocation in more depth. But if we remove the ambiguity then the appearance of validity disappears:

Argument 5.13 (disambiguated):

Premise one: If the premises of argument 5.11 are true, then the conclusion of argument 5.11 *must (empirically)* be true.

Premise two: If an argument is such that if its premises are true its conclusion *must (logically)* be true, then the argument is *valid*.

Conclusion: Argument 5.11 is valid.

This disambiguated argument would be valid only if empirical and logical 'must's coincide. If they don't the argument only appears to be valid. Empirical and logical 'must's do not, of course, coincide. Argument 5.13 is therefore another example of an argument that isn't persuasive even if it is valid and sound.

Argument 5.13 might appear to be sound. But by applying our four step method, and carefully distinguishing empirical possibility from logical possibility we can see that it is either invalid (because the appearance of validity rests on an equivocation), or such that at least one of its premises is false.

Interestingly, given that premise one of argument 5.13 is the conclusion of argument 5.12, we can also see that if premise one of argument 5.13 is false, this means that the conclusion of argument 5.12 is false, and we can be certain - if we weren't already - that at least one of *its* premises is also false.

Deduction

I hope you are impressed by just *how much* you can learn from applying our four step method to a rather complex argument. In particular I hope you are impressed by the clarity that can be achieved on just what is wrong with the argument.

In this case there were rather a lot of things wrong with our interlocutor's argument. You might be feeling anything *but* clear on what is wrong with it. If this is the case work though the sections devoted to the argument again, making sure you understand each step as you come to it.

I promise you there is clarity to be achieved!

We are now at the end of chapter five!

I said at the beginning that by the end you would be able to:

- understand and explain the implications of the definition of validity;

- explain what it is for an argument to preserve, but not to generate, truth;

- explain the procedure for testing deductive arguments;

- understand why this procedure works;

- create counterexample sets for deductive arguments;

- recognise when a counterexample set is consistent or inconsistent;

- explain the implications of the consistency or inconsistency of a counterexample set for the validity of an argument;

- explain why counterexample sets are not arguments;

- recognise arguments that are valid but unpersuasive.

Can you do these things?

If so well done! If not you will be better off going through the relevant steps again before you move onto chapter six.

CHAPTER SIX

Fallacies

This chapter corresponds to the sixth podcast in my series **'Critical Reasoning: A Romp Through the Nature of Arguments'**. The video podcast can be found at metafore.com/CR6video, the audio-only podcast at metafore.com/CR6audio, slides at metafore.com/CR6slides and a transcript at http://mariannetalbot.co.uk/transcripts/.

Unless you are up for the challenge of formal logic, this is the final chapter of the book. Well done for getting this far!

In this chapter we shall be discussing *fallacies*. Fallacies are common patterns of bad reasoning; patterns of *bad* reasoning that look enough like patterns of good reasoning to fool some of the people some of the time. We shall look at what fallacies are, the difficulties of systematising fallacies, and how fallacies can mislead us.

A careful reading of this chapter will enable you to:

- define 'fallacy' and use the words 'fallacy' and 'fallacious' with confidence;

- say why it is important to have a grasp of the nature of a fallacy;

- distinguish two categories of fallacy;

- see that, and why, fallacies are as difficult to systematise as inductive arguments;

- describe and exemplify a few key fallacies;

- know where to go to learn about other fallacies;

- be alert to the contexts in which particular fallacies may lurk;

- try to avoid fallacies in your own arguments;

- better recognise when others' arguments are fallacious.

What is a Fallacy?

We all reason badly sometimes. Maybe we have a terrible cold, our heads are full of cotton wool and we can't think straight. Maybe we are under stress, our thinking has become muddled and we engage in self-deception. Maybe we are overwhelmed by emotion or desire and we engage in wishful thinking. All these situations are ones in which we may reason badly. But faulty reasoning of this kind is not automatically *fallacious*.

Then there are those techniques that are often successfully used in persuasion but which certainly don't count as good reasoning. Sarcasm, irony, spite, kicking sand in someone's face etc., can all be used to win arguments, and one who stoops to these methods might be said to be reasoning badly. Again though, their reasoning is not automatically *fallacious*.

For reasoning to be *fallacious* it must exemplify a *fallacy*.

Fallacies are patterns of faulty reasoning that, because they are so often mistaken for patterns of good reasoning, are common enough to have been identified and named. Fallacies, we might say, are *bad* arguments that look like *good* arguments.

In everyday language people will often say, of a false belief, that it is a fallacy. This is not the way we'll be using the word in this book. Here only a pattern of reasoning, a *type* of argument (or reasoning pattern), can be a fallacy. Particular bad arguments or bad patterns of reasoning, can be said to be *fallacious*, and when they are, that is because they are *instances* of a given fallacy.

Exercise 6.1: Is this a fallacy?

Premise one: Jeffrey Pollack died of a heart attack whilst
                    jogging

Conclusion: Jogging will cause you to have a heart attack.

Answers on page 380

Let's have a quick look at why learning about fallacies is A Good
Thing.

Learning About Fallacies

As you might expect there are *loads* of different fallacies. The
Internet Encyclopaedia of Philosophy (http://www.iep.utm.edu/
fallacy/) names 209! This, however, is partly because its
definition of 'fallacy' is slightly wider than ours - it includes as
fallacies certain forms of false belief, and we are including only
patterns of faulty reasoning.

Learning that there are something like 209 fallacies might prompt
you to think that it will be a nightmare learning them all. You
might even question why you *should* learn about fallacies. You
wouldn't learn about football, after all, by learning how *not* to
handle a ball. You wouldn't learn about cooking by learning how
not to combine your ingredients. Why should learning about
reasoning involve your learning how not to reason?

But acquiring a familiarity with fallacies is an important part of learning how to reason well. In fact in learning anything – including football and cooking - it is always salutary to learn about the common errors people make. These errors are often common for a reason. They are common because we so often take things at face value, failing to question our first instincts. In assuming that whatever instinct tells us is correct is in fact correct we often go wrong.

It can be easy, for example, to mistake a case of the fallacy of affirming the consequent:

Premise one: If P then Q

Premise two: Q

Conclusion: Therefore P.

for a case of the valid argument form, modus ponens:

Premise one: If P then Q

Premise two: P

Conclusion: Therefore Q.

It can be easy to do this because the two argument forms undoubtedly look alike at first glance. We also have a tendency to confuse 'if-then' with 'if and only if'. Can you see that if we read the 'if-then' of the first premises of these arguments as 'if and only if' the arguments would *both* be valid?

But when you know about the fallacy you become alert to the possibility that what you *think* is a case of modus ponens might be a case of affirming the consequent. The very fact you know that you might mistake a given fallacy for a given valid argument form, should make it less likely you'll make that mistake.

Exercise 6.2: Please decide which of the following arguments is a case of affirming the consequent , and which is a valid instance of modus ponens:

1. If it is summer the bees will be pollinating the flowers. The bees are pollinating the flowers. Therefore it is summer.

2. If it is winter many animals will be in hibernations. It is winter. Therefore many animals are in hibernation.

3. If an animal is treated well and has no genetic condition it will thrive. This animal has been treated well and has no genetic condition. Therefore this animal will thrive.

4. If it is spring the snowdrops will be out. The snowdrops are out. Therefore it is spring.

5. If it is summer the bees will be pollinating the flowers. It is summer, Therefore the bees are pollinating the flowers.

6. If the plant is treated well and given the right nutrients it will thrive. The plant is thriving. Therefore the plant is being treated well and given the right nutrients.

Answers on page 381

It can also be easy, if you have independent reason to think that Linda is a feminist, mistakenly to think that the conjunction of two states of affairs:

Linda is a feminist bank teller

is more probable than one of its conjuncts

Linda is a bank teller.

But a moment's thought should tell you that the former *cannot* be more probable than the latter, given that the class of feminist bank tellers is a sub-class of the class of bank tellers. (This example comes from Daniel Kahneman's admirable book Thinking Fast and Slow: http://vk.com/doc23267904_175119602 or http://www.amazon.co.uk/Thinking-Fast-Slow-Daniel-Kahneman/dp/0141033576).

Be careful here: knowing that Linda is a feminist undoubtedly gives you reason to believe that *if* Linda is a bank teller she is a feminist bank teller. But you were asked simply whether Linda's being a feminist bank teller is *more probable* than her being a bank teller. There are states of affairs that obtain despite their being less probable than other states of affairs.

This is an instance of the *conjunction* fallacy. Again your awareness of the possibility of falling into the conjunction fallacy will enable you to guard against this fallacy when asked to judge probabilities.

Exercise 6.4: Anyone familiar with Daniel Kahneman's book *Thinking, Fast and Slow* will see that the following thought experiment is modelled on his 'Linda' and 'Tom W' thought experiments (see especially chapters 14 and 15).

Jane is an active vivacious person with a liking for music and dancing. She always watches Strictly Come Dancing and for exercise she likes to go to Zumba classes (a type of workout in which one makes various dance-like moves to Latin American music).

Please rank in order of probability the subject that Jane is studying at university:

Humanities

Dance

Answers on page 381

Beware Over Confidence!

So it is beneficial to learn about fallacies because, in learning about them, we learn how to guard against them in our own reasoning, and watch for them in the reasoning of others.

We shouldn't, though, make the mistake of thinking that awareness of these fallacies will *immunise* us against these common errors in reasoning.

To see this, let's reflect on the Muller-Lyer illusion. You are probably familiar with this illusion. The question you are asked is whether one of these lines is longer than the other.

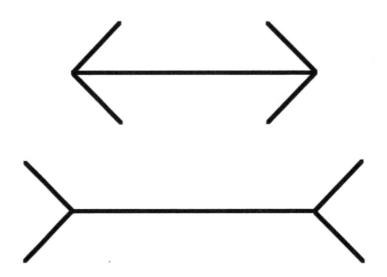

The answer is that the lines are the same length, although the effect of the arrow 'head' and 'tail' is that they *look* extremely different. The line with the 'tails' looks much longer than the line with the 'heads'.

Whether or not you know this illusion you might be interested in this website: http://michaelbach.de/ot/sze_muelue/index.html. This will test your understanding of this thought experiment and offer you some thoughts on how it might be explained. It will also introduce you to many other fascinating optical illusions.

I am drawing your attention to the Muller-Lyer illusion because, whilst an understanding of the illusion will enable you to guard against knee-jerk judgements to the effect that the lines differ in length, it won't stop the lines from *looking* different lengths. The illusion persists even after you have become aware it *is* an illusion.

Something similar is true in the case of fallacies. You may think that knowledge of the difference between affirming the consequent and modus ponens will immunise you against mistaking one for the other, but unless you pay careful attention to the argument in front of you, you may find that you can *still* be fooled. The same is true of the conjunction fallacy.

The only reliable way of eradicating fallacies from your own reasoning, and being able to recognise them in the reasoning of others, is to expend time and effort in guarding against these fallacies. You can only do this, however, if you have made yourself aware of the various fallacies in advance: knowing where they lurk is vital in the attempt to guard against them.

Fallacies that might not be Fallacious

Fallacies, I said at the beginning of this chapter, are bad arguments that can easily be mistaken for good arguments. But actually this definition needs to be modified. There are arguments that are, or seem to be, instances of fallacies, but that are not at all obviously bad arguments.

For example, if I tell you that you shouldn't listen to arguments offered by Fred because Fred is known to be notoriously mistaken in all his views, then we have, apparently, a case of the fallacy of *ad hominem*. I am arguing against *Fred* rather than *Fred's argument*. This is supposed to be disallowed.

But should it be? If Fred really is notoriously mistaken in all his views then isn't listening to him a waste of your time?

The canonical answer to this is that, on this occasion, Fred's views might be worth listening to: my ad hominem attack on him cannot detract from that possibility.

On the other hand, though, given that we have finite time to listen to or read others' arguments, aren't I still right to say that listening to Fred is a waste of your time? If so then my ad hominem attack strikes home, doesn't it, despite being an instance of a fallacy?

Another fallacy some instances of which appear to be *good* arguments is the *slippery slope* fallacy. It really *is* the case that allowing yourself to procrastinate on a few occasions could put you at the top of a slippery slope to moral turpitude and a wasted life. Aristotle might well have been right to say that the virtues are a matter of habits; the first lie, after all, is difficult, the second much easier.

On the other hand, there are many people who believe that changing the law to allow voluntary euthanasia might eventually result in our legalising *non*-voluntary or even *in*voluntary euthanasia.

But we might say this supposed slippery slope is not so obviously slippery. Why, given that new legislation would be needed at each point, should we accept that legalising *voluntary euthanasia* will result, willy nilly, in legalising *non-voluntary euthanasia*?

Some slippery slope arguments can be defused quite quickly by our pointing to some principled way to halt the slide. Others are not so easily defused.

Some of those who work on fallacies hope that we will eventually find a principled way to distinguish between arguments that *are* fallacious, and those that aren't, within a given category. Others, though, suspect that the distinction is *extra-logical*, that we have to look to pragmatics, to our society, or to human nature, to work out why some instances do not appear fallacious. For example it has been said that ad hominem attacks are acceptable so long as the attack is *relevant*. Relevance, of course, is notoriously hard to systematise as you will see if you would like to read the first three paragraphs of this amusing paper by philosopher Daniel Dennett: http://www.cs.sfu.ca/~vaughan/teaching/415/papers/dennett-cognitivewheels.html

Two Systems of Thought?

Daniel Kahneman explains the fact you can still be fooled even though you know about fallacies and illusions by distinguishing two systems of thought. He calls these 'system one' and 'system two'.

System one thinking is fast, automatic and effortless. It is this sort of thinking that gets you home on those occasions when you realise, having parked the car, that you have spent the whole journey in a pleasant daydream about your next holiday.

System two thinking is slower because it requires effort and attention. It is this sort of thinking that wears you out when you have driven home on a dark night, through lashing rain and heavy traffic. This is the sort of thinking you have been engaged in (I hope) whilst reading this book.

Kahneman explains that when asked a question about the probability of Linda's being a feminist bank teller or a bank teller, having been told that Linda is a feminist, your system one will rush to answer that the former is more probable than the latter. It is your system two that will rein in the rush and suggest you pay more attention to your answer, and in particular to the rules of probability theory.

Kahneman has a great deal of interesting and highly convincing empirical evidence for his distinction between system one thinking and system two thinking.

A Wanton Will?

A similar distinction, however, was made by the philosopher Descartes in *The Meditations On First Philosophy*, which was published in 1641: metafore.com/cr/med1.

If you'd like to *listen* to the Meditations, you'll find an audio version here: https://librivox.org/meditations-on-first-philosophy-by-rene- descartes/

In Meditation IV Descartes explains the fact that we so often fall into error in making judgements by saying that our will is more extensive than our understanding. We exercise our will, says Descartes, in wantonly assenting to beliefs as they're 'put to us', without taking the time and trouble to subject them to criticism. If we were to subject them to conscious criticism before assenting to them we would *not*, he says, fall into error.

So when we look at the Muller-Lyer lines our faculty of perception clearly 'puts to us' the belief that the lines differ in length. A naïve subject might respond at face value to the belief that is 'put to him' by assenting to it; by making a *judgement* to the effect that the lines differ in length. His judgement would, of course, be false.

A non-naïve subject will, however, withhold consent, in order to look more closely at the lines, to see whether this is a classic case of Muller-Lyer (where the lines are the same length) or whether this is in fact a double bluff (where the lines are not the same length). A sensible person (with a lot of time to spare) might even take a ruler to the lines in order to make his judgement. The judgement of this person is much more likely to be true.

But the non-naïve subject is still subject to the illusion. His perceptual systems still 'put to him' the belief that the lines differ in length. The difference is that he withholds assent to this belief. He refuses to take things at face value. He is prepared to put in the time and effort required to avoid error.

It is easy, I think, to see in the Cartesian distinction, made 350 years ago, a similar distinction to that between Kahneman's 'system one thinking' and 'system two thinking'. The 'system' that assents to whatever is put to it corresponds to system one thinking. The 'system' that insists on taking a more critical approach corresponds to system two thinking.

Of course Descartes was not engaged in empirical research when he was writing his Meditations. His methodology was entirely philosophical: he was reflecting on the operations of his own mind. There is nothing scientific about his findings. In particular there is no evidence on which to generalise them to others. Nevertheless, it is interesting, I think, to find Kahneman's empirical studies bearing out Descartes's conclusions.

Fallacies Again

So knowing about the fallacies of conjunction and affirming the consequent won't stop your mistaking instances of these fallacies for the real thing. There is no substitute for putting in the mental effort and attention you need to guard against such mistakes. Engaging 'system two' thinking, or subjecting to critical scrutiny the beliefs that are 'put to you', is essential if you are to avoid faulty reasoning.

But if you do put in this effort and attention, it will undoubtedly become easier both to recognise these mistakes in the reasoning of others, and to avoid them in your own reasoning. So it is worth learning about fallacies, so you can consciously guard against them.

Systematising Fallacies

You may remember that when, in chapter five, we looked at deductive arguments, we found that they can always be classified as good or bad, depending upon whether or not they satisfy the definition of validity. The definition of validity is the same for all deductive arguments.

When we looked at inductive arguments in chapter four, however, we found them frustratingly difficult to systematise. We can say, at the highest level of generality, that the more probable the conclusion of an inductive argument given the truth of its premises, the better the argument is. But the question of how probable a conclusion is made by a set of premises differs from one type of inductive argument to another.

All we can do, in learning how to reason inductively, is to learn what counts as the key criteria for a good argument with respect to each of the different types of inductive arguments.

Fallacies are more like inductive arguments than deductive. It is extremely difficult – perhaps even impossible – to systematise them. This means that there is no real substitute for looking at each of the fallacies individually and learning why it is a fallacy, the context in which it makes its characteristic appearances, and how, therefore, it might best be avoided.

Over the centuries many have tried to categorise them. The first such attempt (so far as we know) was that of Aristotle. In 350 BCE he wrote *De Sophistical Elenchis*.

If you would like to check out what Aristotle says about fallacies you can access *De Sophistical Elenchis* online here: http://classics.mit.edu/Aristotle/sophist_refut.html (Warning: Aristotle was known to the ancients as a wonderfully clear writer, but all we have are his lecture notes. These do not show his 'wonderfully clear' writing at its best).

In chapter four of this book he identifies 13 fallacies, classifying them under two headings: those dependent upon language and those 'outside' language. Here is Aristotle's classification:

Sophistical Refutations Outside Language:

Accident;

The use of words absolutely or in a certain respect;

Misconception of refutation;

Assumption of the original point;

Consequent;

Non-cause as cause;

The making of more than one question into one.

Sophistical Refutations Dependent on Language:

Ambiguity (or Equivocation);

Amphiboly;

Composition;

Division;

Accent;

Form of Expression

Other philosophers have tried their best to make sense of the fallacies, both formal and informal, by sub-dividing them into further categories. In an earlier version of my critical reasoning podcasts , for example, I relied on a classification used by Robert J. Fogelin in his book Understanding Arguments: An Introduction to Informal Logic (http://www.amazon.co.uk/Understanding-Arguments-Introduction-Informal-Logic/dp/0155075489)

In this book Fogelin talks of fallaciesof *clarity* (slippery slopes, heaps, borderline cases, scaling adjectives, ambiguity and definition), *relevance* (ad hominem, authority , appeal to pity, affirming the consequent) and *vacuity* (circularity, question-begging).

The website Fallacy Files offers a comprehensive taxonomy of fallacies at: metafore.com/cr/fallacies.

None of these classifications should be accepted uncritically. This means that you should use whichever one suits you (if there is one that suits you) in the safe knowledge that you can ignore the rest! If no classification appeals then ignore them all!

Aristotle's two-fold distinction, however, has come down to us through the years as a distinction between *formal* fallacies and *informal* fallacies. I find this distinction fairly useful and shall say a bit more about each category of fallacy.

Formal Fallacies

We have come across the distinction between form and content several times in this book. In chapter two, for example, we discussed removing the content of an argument and revealing its form, when we discussed analysing arguments. In chapter three we discussed it again when discussing interpretations and in particular when we saw that deductive arguments can be evaluated a priori, whereas inductive arguments can be evaluated only a posteriori. In chapter five we discussed it again whilst discussing the evaluation of deductive arguments. In chapter seven (if you get that far!) we shall discuss it again in discussing formalising arguments.

But here we come across the distinction between form and content in distinguishing *formal* fallacies from *informal* fallacies.

Formal fallacies (or, in Aristotle's terminology those 'outside' language) are those that depend upon the *structure* or *form* of an argument. It is not quite true to say that such fallacies have nothing to do with language, because they depend on the logical words of the arguments, their meanings and the way they are combined. But they don't have anything to do with the language of an argument *other* than the logical language of that argument.

The fallacy *affirming the consequent,* which we have already encountered, is a formal fallacy. *Any* argument with the form:

Premise one: If P then Q

Premise two: Q

Conclusion: Therefore P.

will be an instance of this fallacy, whatever it is about. Similarly, of course, any argument of the form If P then Q, P, therefore Q will be an instance of modus ponens, and so valid. Another formal fallacy is the fallacy of denying the antecedent. Here is the form of this fallacy:

Premise one: If P then Q

Premise two: It is not the case that P

Conclusion: It is not the case that Q.

This argument is easily mistaken for the valid argument form called *modus tollens*:

Premise one: If P then Q

Premise two: It is not the case that Q

Conclusion: It is not the case that P.

Can you see that whilst the latter, the *valid* argument form, in the second premise, denies the *consequent* of the conditional in the first premise, the fallacy, in the second premise, denies the *antecedent* of that conditional.

To fail to see the fallacy might prompt someone to think that an argument like the following is valid:

Premise one: If he is her brother then he is male

Premise two: It is not the case that he is her brother

Conclusion: It is not the case he is male.

because they are mistaking it for an argument like this:

Premise one: If he is her brother then he is male

Premise two: It is not the case that he is male

Conclusion: It is not the case he is her brother.

Whilst Aristotle lists only seven formal fallacies we now recognise many more of them. To get a feel for them you might look at the taxonomy offered by the Fallacy Files under 'Formal Fallacies': http://www.fallacyfiles.org/formfall.html.

It is easy to think of formal fallacies as deductive fallacies. But this would be a mistake. There are formal fallacies that are not errors in deductive reasoning. For example the conjunction fallacy is not an error of deductive reasoning, but an error of inductive reasoning. Arguably, though, it is a formal fallacy because it violates the formal rules of probability theory. (Be careful here, the Fallacy Files gives the impression that formal fallacies are deductive, and informal fallacies inductive, despite the fact it classifies many arguments from probability in the 'formal' category).

I have introduced you to several different formal fallacies. But if you'd like to know more about formal fallacies then I advise you to spend some time on the Fallacy Files website familiarising yourself with the many different formal fallacies.

Informal Fallacies

An *informal* fallacy, or in Aristotle's terminology, a fallacy 'dependent on language' is, as you might imagine, a fallacy that depends upon the content, or non-logical language, of an argument, not just its form.

The fallacy of *equivocation*, for example, is an informal fallacy because to recognise an equivocation we must take into account the non-logical language in which an argument is couched.

When we go to strip the content out of this argument, for example, to replace it with 'P's and 'Q's, we should find ourselves hesitating:

Premise one: Criminal actions are illegal

Premise two: All murder trials are criminal actions

Conclusion: All murder trials are illegal.

The 'knee-jerk' way of stripping this argument of content would be:

Premise one: As are B

Premise two: All Cs are As

Conclusion: All Cs are B.

But this will not do. The exercise below gives you an opportunity to work out why not.

What is the problem that should cause us to
hesitate in formalising this argument in the
manner suggested?

Answer on page 382

Normal English speakers with their wits about them (those who
are exercising their 'system two' mode of thinking!) will see
immediately that to translate 'criminal action' in the same way in
each of these premises would be a mistake. Once this mistake has
been made, however, the formal language of the argument
obscures the error. The argument, translated as we translated it
above, is formally valid.

The error lies in the translation. Anyone translating it thus missed
the fact that a given phrase was used in two quite different ways.
They missed, that is, an equivocation.

The argument is better translated:

Premise one: As are B

Premise two: All Cs are D

Conclusion: All Cs are B.

It should be clear that this is *not* a valid argument form.

Another example of an informal fallacy is the fallacy of *The Straw
Man*. An example of this fallacy is found whenever someone
interprets something someone else says in way that makes it sound
obviously wrong.

237

In my lectures on critical reasoning I used this example of the Straw Man fallacy:

Jim: Sunny days are good

Sally: If it never rained we'd all starve to death

Strictly speaking Jim isn't making an argument at all, so Sally's riposte can't be regarded as an attempt to refute his argument. But we can eke out Jim's statement as:

Premise one: Sunny days are good

Premise two: Today is sunny

Conclusion: Today is good.

Having done this we can then see Sally's riposte as an attempt to undermine Jim's argument by undermining his first premise.

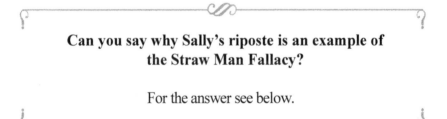

**Can you say why Sally's riposte is an example of
the Straw Man Fallacy?**

For the answer see below.

If you were Jim you'd probably be irritated by Sally's reply. After all you haven't said that the *only* good days are sunny days, or that sunny days suffice for life, or that avoiding starvation depends on *all* our days being sunny, or any of the other things that would make Sally's riposte relevant.

Sally is making a caricature of Jim's argument. She is interpreting it as something like:

Premise one: The *only* good days are sunny days

Premise two: Today is a sunny day

Conclusion: Today is a good day.

So interpreted it is, of course, quite easy to knock down, especially if we interpret the word 'good' as meaning 'good for human health' rather than 'good for my enjoyment' which is probably more the meaning Jim intended.

Instances of straw men fallacies are *hugely* common. In chapter one (page 35), we discussed the Principle of Charity. I recommended the Principle of Charity to you as a way of avoiding errors in reasoning. In using it you must always treat your opponent's apparent falsehoods and stupidities as evidence for *your* error (have you misunderstood him? Has he mis-spoken? Might *your* belief be false?).

In constructing straw men of your opponents' arguments you are ignoring the Principle of Charity; you are making your opponents' argument seem stupider then it is and so easier to refute.

If your audience fails to notice this, of course, you might 'win' the argument. But logically speaking you have simply ignored their argument. In studying critical reasoning your aim, presumably, is to learn to reason well. In pursuit of that aim the straw man is a particularly important fallacy to avoid.

Your aim, in fact, should be to construct, on your opponent's behalf, the *strongest* possible version of his argument. If you can refute *this* version of his argument you are leaving your opponent without a leg to stand on. Refuting a straw man is easy. Your opponent is left untouched.

In academic philosophy, readers of a paper will often come across a philosopher pointing out a problem with his opponent's argument, and then reconstructing the argument *without* the problem. Only then do they address the argument. They do this because they know that refuting an argument with an error in it is no cause for celebration. If they can show the argument fails even once the error is corrected then the celebration can start!

If what you are after is *truth* or *knowledge* rather than the appearance (to those who haven't noticed your construction of a straw man) of having won an argument, this is the way to go.

Informal Fallacies and Induction

Again it may be tempting to think that informal fallacies are *inductive* fallacies. Again, though, you would be wrong. There are informal fallacies that are deductive in form. For example, any circular argument can be represented as a deductively valid argument. Again the fallacy can be detected only by understanding the *non-logical* language.

For example, consider this argument:

Premise one: It is always wrong to kill human babies

Premise two: Therapeutic cloning involves killing human babies

Conclusion: Therapeutic cloning is wrong.

It is question-begging because anyone who would accept the first premise of the argument would also accept the conclusion.

But if we were to represent this argument as follows:

Premise one: P is always wrong

Premise two: Therapeutic cloning involves P

Conclusion: Therapeutic cloning is wrong.

The fact that the argument begs the question is obscured.

In order to see the fault in the reasoning, one has to understand that we cannot assume that the very early foetuses that are undoubtedly killed in therapeutic cloning, can obviously be called 'human babies'. Premise one is arguably true if by 'killing human babies' we mean 'killing human babies', premise two is only true if by 'killing human babies' we mean 'killing human foetuses'. The two are not obviously equivalent in meaning, and the argument:

Premise one: It is always wrong to kill human babies

Premise two: Therapeutic cloning involves killing human foetuses

Conclusion: Therapeutic cloning is wrong.

is clearly not valid.

I have now introduced you to several informal fallacies. But if you'd like to know more informal fallacies then again I advise you to spend some time on the Fallacy Files website, familiarising yourself this time with the many informal fallacies: http://www.fallacyfiles.org/inforfal.html.

I said above that there is no substitute for learning about the different individual fallacies. It would take up far too much space in this book to do that here. There is also no need to do it. The generous Gary N. Curtis of the Fallacy Files is happy, instead, to let me point you in the direction of his useful website. I advise you, therefore, to access that website and have a good rummage around.

> *Go onto the websiteThe Fallacy Files and have a look around http://www.fallacyfiles.org/index.html*

In case you would like to try other websites, here are some more options:

http://philosophy.lander.edu/logic/fallacy_topics.html

https://yourlogicalfallacyis.com/

Well, that's it for fallacies! I said at the beginning of this chapter that a careful reading of it would enable you to:

- define 'fallacy' and use the words 'fallacy' and 'fallacious' with confidence;

- say why it is important to have a grasp of the nature of a fallacy;

- distinguish two categories of fallacy;

- see that, and why, fallacies are as difficult to systematise as inductive arguments;

- describe and exemplify a few key fallacies;

- know where to go to learn about other fallacies;

- be alert to the contexts in which particular fallacies may lurk;

- try to avoid fallacies in your own arguments;

- better recognise when others' arguments are fallacious.

I hope that this is indeed the case!

Well, that is now it, unless you are interested in learning how to formalise arguments, and how to test them 'mechanically' by means of the rules of propositional logic. If this is not your bag, then please don't think the less of yourself. Many of those interested in critical reasoning, are not *so* interested that they want to learn about formal logic. If this describes you, then we can now part company.

I do hope you have enjoyed this book. I should be delighted to know whether you have or you haven't. There is a facility for getting in touch with me on my website: www.mariannetalbot.co.uk and of course you can always direct message me on twitter: @oxphil_marianne or come to my Facebook page Marianne Talbot Philosophy. I should be particularly interested if you have caught me in some sort of error – the nice thing about e-books (and print on demand books) is that such errors can be dealt with quite quickly! Please help me by letting me know if you have caught something.

Otherwise goodbye, and good luck with all your future reasoning! If you are interested in learning how to formalise arguments and how to test them with the rules of propositional logic , then we travel on together....

CHAPTER SEVEN

Formalising Arguments

This chapter corresponds to podcast two in the series: A Romp Through the Foothills of Logic. This is available in audio only and you'll find it at metafore.com/CR7audio1. There is also a short (15 minute) video podcast on formalising arguments that you will find at metafore.com/CRFormalisingArguments. The slides are at metafore.com/CR7slides and the transcripts at mariannetalbot.co.uk/transcripts.

I really do recommend you listen to the podcasts for this chapter and the next – there are many concepts and activities that will be completely new to you. Many people find them very hard when first presented with them and the podcasts will talk you through them so you can actually *see* me doing the things I am talking about.

This chapter and the next are entirely optional – if you are not interested in learning about how to formalise arguments into the language of propositional logic (henceforth 'PL'), and how to test them by applying the rules of PL then you finished the book when you finished chapter six! This chapter, and the next, deal with *formal* rather than *informal* logic. Many people find this really hard and unless you are really prepared to put in an effort why not just skip them?

Still with me? Great!

Determining the validity of arguments by applying the rules of PL depends on the ability to translate English arguments into the language of PL This involves acquiring four abilities:

Ability One: distinguish those arguments we can formalise in the language of PL from those we can't (pages 248-258);

Ability Two: provide an interpretation by allocating sentence letters to the simple declarative sentences constituting the relevant English arguments (pages 258-266);

Ability Three: identify the correct symbols to represent the truth-functional connectives from which the complex sentences of the relevant English arguments are constituted (pages 266-285);

Ability Four: represent English argument claims as sequents of PL (pages 286-288).

This is what we'll be learning in *this* chapter. By the time you have carefully read this chapter you will be able to:

- recognise those arguments to which PL applies;

- use the truth-table test to identify truth-functional sentence connectives;

- explain the truth-table definitions of all the truth functors of PL;

- explain why truth-tables represent meanings;

- make use of brackets to indicate the scope of truth functional connectives;

- translate sentences into well-formed formulae (wffs – pronounced 'woof's) of PL;

- avoid the pitfalls of translating English sentences into wffs;

- formalise English argument claims into semantic and syntactic sequents

- explain the meaning of such sequents.

At the end of the chapter we'll pause for you to reflect on whether you can indeed do these things.

But now let's look at each of the four abilities in turn.

Ability One: Distinguishing the Arguments that can be Formalised

First we'll consider the limitations of PL. When you see what it *can't* do you may question its power. Without PL, though, computation would be impossible. It really is extremely powerful.

PL cannot be used to test:

(a) inductive arguments;

(b) deductive arguments whose validity depends on anything other than their propositional structure;

(c) deductive arguments that depend on non-truth-functional sentence connectives.

Let's have a look at each.

Limitation One: Induction

PL is useless when it comes to induction. This means PL cannot evaluate arguments that rely on *empirical* (as opposed to logical) necessity, arguments that deal with *contingencies.* That's a lot of arguments it can't deal with.

The project of formalising induction is still on the starting blocks compared to the project of formalising deduction. We have made great strides with statistics and Probability Theory but neither is as systematic or generalisable as the system by which we formalise deductive arguments. It is not obvious it ever will be.

But even if PL can't be used with induction, this doesn't impugn it as a means of formalising and testing deductive arguments. Arguments that turn on *logical* necessity are important.

Limitation Two: . Propositional Structure

When I started this book I had to decide whether to talk of argument-constituents as *sentences*, *statements* or *propositions*. I decided to talk about sentences.

But now we are talking about *PL* and discussing *propositional* structure, you should know about statements and propositions.

Propositions, Statements and Declarative Sentences

We both *use* and *mention* sentences. You'll remember this from chapter one. A sentence being mentioned is called a 'declarative sentence', one that is being *used* is called a 'statement'. So if I use the declarative sentence 'the dress is red', I make the statement *the dress is red.* In doing this I am expressing the *proposition* [the dress is red].

A proposition is the content of a belief. One and the same proposition can be expressed by different sentences. So 'La robe est rouge' and 'The dress is red' are two different *sentences* which, in use make different statements. But both can be used to express the same *proposition* (if they are about the same dress).

Here are the definitions of 'statement' and 'proposition':

> **Def:** a *statement* is a sentence in use.

> **Def:** a *proposition* is the content of the belief expressed by a statement.

In chapter one we defined 'declarative sentence' as a sentence that could be used to make an assertion. To use a sentence with assertoric force to express a belief is to make a statement. The words 'statement' and 'assertion', therefore, are being used interchangeably.

Thought and language are intertwined. We use sentences to express beliefs. To reason is to move rationally from belief to belief. Arguments are the linguistic expression of our reasoning.

If animals can think, there must be thought without language. But can animals think? Check this out here: http://plato.stanford.edu/entries/concepts/#ConN atLan

---

Propositional Structure

The validity of some deductive arguments depends entirely on their propositional structure. Here is one:

Argument 7.1:

Premise one: If it is Friday then Marianne is wearing jeans

Premise two: It is Friday

Conclusion: Marianne is wearing jeans.

There is no need to look *inside* the simple sentences of argument 7.1 to determine its validity. Each *simple* sentence stands as an unanalysed whole. The validity of argument 7.1 turns *solely* on the sentences that constitute it, together with the fact its complex sentence (premise one) is constructed out of simple sentences and the phrase 'if/then', which connects two of the sentences.

Predicate Structure

Here, though, is a deductive argument the validity of which depends on something *other* than its propositional structure:

Argument 7.2:

Premise one: Marianne is wearing jeans

Premise two: Marianne is the Director of Studies in Philosophy at OUDCE

Conclusion: The Director of Studies in Philosophy at OUDCE is wearing jeans.

It is only by looking *inside* the simple sentences of argument 7.2 that we can determine its validity. Its validity turns, in part, on the way in which its sentences are constituted of sub-sentential parts (predicates – words for properties, and designators, words referring to individuals). The validity of this argument turns on its *predicate* structure.

It is a necessary condition of using PL to formalise and test an argument that the validity of that argument depends *entirely* on its propositional structure.

PL can't even help us with *all* deductive arguments. Argument 7.1 it can manage. Argument 7.2 it can't. (This doesn't mean that argument 7.2 can't be formalised at all – but you'd need predicate logic, which is the next one up from the propositional logic that you're doing.)

Nevertheless in learning PL you are learning the building blocks of *all* formalisation.

Limitation Three: Truth Functionality

We can formalise and test, by means of PL, *only* those deductive
arguments the validity of which turns on sentence connectives that
are *truth-functional.*

A truth-functional connective is a species of sentence connective.
A sentence connective – er – connects sentences; it takes one or
more sentences to make another sentence.

English has many sentence connectives. Here are a few:

a.   P and Q;

b.   it is probably the case that P;

c.   P or Q;

d.   P because Q;

e.   it is not the case that P;

f.   it is necessarily the case that P.

Each of these words or phrases takes one or more declarative sentences (represented by 'P' and 'Q') and uses them to make another sentence.

Unary and Binary Connectives

It might seem odd to call 'it is probably the case that P' (and 'it is not the case that P' and 'it is necessarily the case that P') *connectives*. They don't *connect* anything, each takes *one* sentence and turns it into another.

Nevertheless it *is* called a 'connective'. It is a *unary connective*. When a connective takes two sentences as most do, they are called *binary connectives*.

Sentence connectives are sometimes called 'sentence-functors' after mathematical functions. Sentence functors take sentences as 'arguments', and generate new sentences as 'values'. Sentence connectives are also called 'operators' because they operate on sentences to produce new sentences. By analogy truth-functional connectives can be called either 'truth-functors' or 'truth-functional operators'.

As PL works only on arguments whose validity turns on truth-functional operators we must learn to recognise when a connective is truth-functional.

Truth Functional Connectives

A sentence connective is truth-functional when and only when the truth value of any sentence built from it is a function *solely* of the truth values of its constituent sentences.

The sentence connective 'and' is truth-functional whenever it connects sentence. It takes two sentences to make a third. The third sentence is called the *conjunction* of the other two sentences. The truth value of the conjunction depends entirely on the truth values of its constituent sentences.

We can illustrate this by conjoining two simple sentences:

    1)   The cat is on the mat.

and

    2)   The dog is in its basket.

This gives us:

    3)   The cat is on the mat and the dog is in its basket.

The truth value of sentence 3) is determined entirely by the truth value of sentences 1) and 2) as you'll see if you answer the following questions:

(i) if sentence 1) is true and sentence 2) is true, then sentence 3) is......?

(ii) if sentence 1) is true and sentence 2) is false, then sentence 3) is......?

(iii) if sentence 1) is false and sentence 2) is true, then sentence 3) is......?

(iv) if sentence 1) is false and sentence 2) is false, then sentence 3) is ......?

Truth-table Definitions

If we substitute 'P' for sentence 1), and 'Q' for sentence 2), the following is a tabular representation of the truth conditions of sentence 3).

Read the first row as representing the situation in which 'P' and 'Q' are both true, the second row as representing the situation in which 'P' is true and 'Q' is false, and so on. The truth values assigned to 'P and Q' will be the same, I hope, as your answers to the questions above.

P	Q	(P and Q)
T	T	T
T	F	F
F	T	F
F	F	F

If we leave the 'P' and the 'Q' uninterpreted this is a tabular representation of *all* the possible conditions under which *any* sentence constructed by means of 'and' is true and false. It is called a 'truth-table':

Def: **a *truth-table* is a tabular representation of a complete set of truth conditions.**

This truth-table shows that when 'and' is used as a sentence connective (rather than a predicate-connective, as in 'the cat is black and white', something we'll discuss further below) it always makes the same contribution to the meaning of the resulting sentence.

The contribution it makes is the *meaning* of 'and'. The truth-table is, in effect, the *definition* of 'and' used as a sentence connective.

It is a definition because in telling us the truth value of 'and' in *every* possible situation, it tells us *all* the conditions under which sentences connected by 'and' are true and false. This is tantamount to giving us the *meaning* of 'and'.

Be careful. Each row gives the truth value of 'and' only in *one* possible world. You need *the whole truth-table* to get the truth value of 'and' in *every* possible world. It is the latter that is needed for the *meaning* of 'and'.

Non-Truth-Functional Connectives

If the validity of an argument turns on a non-truth-functional sentence connective, you cannot formalise or test it by means of PL. Most English sentence connectives are *not* truth functional. A non-truth-functional connective is a connective that has an incomplete or even an empty truth-table.

For example, the sentence connective 'It is probably the case that' is a non-truth-functional connective. We can demonstrate this as follows:

P	It is probably the case that P
T	?
F	?

We cannot complete the first row of this truth-table because knowing that P is true tells us *nothing* about the truth of 'it is probably the case that P'. The fact that P is true, does *not* entail that P is *probable*. Improbable states of affairs, after all, sometimes obtain.

Knowing that P is false, on the other hand, tells us nothing about the truth of 'it is probably the case that P'. Probable things sometimes *don't* happen.

Knowing the truth value of 'P', therefore, doesn't enable us to determine the truth value of 'it is probably the case that P'. The latter, therefore, is not a truth-functional connective. The truth value of a sentence constituted by it is *not* a function *solely* of the truth value of its constituent sentence.

Any argument the validity of which turns on this sentence connective cannot be formalised or tested by PL.

This *doesn't* mean *any* occurrence of 'probably' prevents an argument from being formalisable. If the 'probably' appears *within* a sentence and the argument doesn't turn on it, then the sentence can be formalised by a sentence letter. We'll look at this below (see page 265).

Exercise 7.2: Can you say which of these sentence
connectives is truth functional and give complete,
partial or blank truth-tables as appropriate?

1. P or Q;

2. P because Q;

3. it is not the case that P;

4. it is necessarily the case that P;

Answers on page 383

Ability Two: Sentence Letters and Interpretations

Translating from English into a formal language is no more
straightforward than translating from one natural language into
another. Sometimes things can be said in one language but not in
another. At other times things can be said, but not as well.

For example, one can say things in Mandarin (I'm told) that
cannot be said in French. English people use the German word
'Zeitgeist' ('spirit of the time') and the Latin expression 'sine qua
non' ('without which nothing') because they usefully capture
something English cannot capture as well.

Logical languages have advantages over natural languages. For
example they don't permit ambiguity. But they cannot capture
everything that can be captured by a natural language. We shall
learn these limitations below. But first we must learn how to
provide an interpretation. This involves allocating sentence letters
to the declarative sentences constituting an argument.

Sentence Letters

We are familiar with sentence letters. We have used them several times in this book already. We used them in chapter three (pages 114-116) to talk about the fact that deductive arguments can be evaluated a priori and in chapter five (page 202) to demonstrate that the validity of an argument is a matter of structure, not content, and to make it easier to determine the consistency of a counterexample set. We also used them above to talk about the truth-functionality of 'and'.

Sentence letters (letters that stand for *sentences*) are always upper case letters. This is purely a convention. Each sentence interpreted must pass the 'frame test' for a declarative sentence. You might have to fiddle with the grammar to make this the case. You mustn't, though, do anything that changes the meaning of the sentence.

I tend to use 'P', 'Q', 'R' etc., but you can use whichever letters take your fancy. Many philosophers would use 'C' (for 'cat') for sentence 1 (on page 254), and 'D' (for 'dog') for sentence 2.

Each sentence letter in an interpretation stands for a different sentence. If that sentence letter is used twice in formalising the argument or a counterexample set, this is because the sentence for which it stands *appears* twice in the argument or the counterexample set.

Interpretations

In chapter two (page 116) we also provided an *interpretation*; a key telling us which sentence letters are allocated to which declarative sentences. You can check this out by looking at the answers to exercise 5.6. (on page 376)

By convention an interpretation is laid out with the sentence letter on the left, followed immediately by a colon, a space and then the English sentence for which the sentence letter stands.

We do not need interpretations to apply the rules of PL. But we do need them to appreciate the import of having applied these rules.

If our application of these rules to an argument tells us that its counterexample set is consistent , we know the argument is invalid. Lacking an interpretation, this is *all* we'd know. With an interpretation we can say, in English, exactly what this counterexample is.

In this chapter and the next we shall be doing exercises with formulae for which no interpretation is provided. These exercises will help you learn the language and rules of PL. In 'real life' you would have no interest in formalised arguments without interpretations; they have *no* meaning.

Exercise 7.3: Provide an interpretation and substitute the appropriate sentence letters for the sentences of the target argument.

Premise one: The economy is not flourishing

Premise two: Herr Kohl is humiliated

Premise three: Herr Kohl will not get grass roots support if Herr Kohl is humiliated

Premise four: Unless Herr Kohl gets grass roots support, the German Government will only last if the economy flourishes

Conclusion: The German Government won't last.

Answers on page 385

Ambiguity

In formalising an argument we must always remove ambiguities. You will remember that argument 5.13 of chapter five traded on the ambiguity of 'must'. We have already seen that argument 5.13 can't be formalised using the language of PL. But if it could you would have to formalise the two senses of 'must' differently.

When formalising English arguments in the language of PL , the ambiguity you will hit most often is structural. Here is a structurally ambiguous sentence:

4)   Jem will go to the party or Sue will go to the party and James will stay at home.

This sentence could mean either:

a)   Jem will go to the party or Sue will go to the party, and James will stay at home.

or

b)   Jem will go to the party, or Sue will go to the party and James will stay at home.

In 4a) James will stay at home *whoever goes to the party*. In 4b) James will stay at home only if *Jem* goes to the party.

If we try to formalise this sentence without regard for this ambiguity, then, on this interpretation:

P: Jem will go to the party

Q: Sue will go to the party

R: James will stay at home

we would get this string of sentence letters and truth functors:

5)   P or Q and R

Unsurprisingly this string is ambiguous. Formally speaking this means that it is not well-formed. To become well-formed it needs brackets.

Where sentence 4) was disambiguated with commas, string 5) can be disambiguated only with brackets. This is the way formal logic expresses the meaning that commas have in English.

Brackets and Scope

Brackets are used to capture the 'scope' of the truth-functional connectives. For example in 4a) the scope of the truth functor 'or' is just 'Sue will go to the party' ('Q'), not 'Sue will go to the party and James will stay at home' ('Q and R'). The scope of the truth-functor 'or' is therefore smaller than that of the 'and':

We show that this is the case by means of brackets.

First we bracket 'P or Q' to show that *it* is a complex sentence. Then we add 'and R' after the brackets, and bracket the whole formula. This gives us:

   5a) ((P or Q) and R)

In 4b) the scope of the 'or' is larger than that of the 'and'. To formalise this we first bracket the 'Q and R', then we add 'P or' before the brackets. Again we bracket the whole formula. This gives us:

   5b) (P or (Q and R))

Exercise 7.4

The following partially formalised sentence: 'Unless R, S only if P' was the result of applying an interpretation to the sentence: "Unless Herr Kohl gets grass roots support, the German Government will only last if the economy flourishes". Can you put brackets into the formalisation to show the scope of the truth functional connectives?

Answers on page 386

Brackets are important. By means of them we can ensure that well-formed formulae of PL are *never* ambiguous. A poet wouldn't see this as an advantage. A logician does.

Exercise 7.5: Can you add brackets to show the ambiguity of the following strings?

1. P and R or S

2. If P then R or S

3. Not P and Q

4. If P then not R or S

Answers on page 386

Non-Truth-Functional Connectives and Scope

PL cannot be used when the validity of an argument turns on a sentence connective that isn't truth-functional.

We saw that 'it is probably the case that P' is not truth-functional. But this doesn't mean that any occurrence of 'probably' in an argument means that the argument cannot be formalised.

The word 'probably' appears in arguments three *and* four. One of these can be formalised, the other can't. Can you say which and why?

Argument 7.3:

Premise one: It is probably the case that Marianne is wearing jeans

Premise two: If it is probably the case that Marianne is wearing jeans then it is Friday.

Conclusion: Therefore it is Friday.

Argument 7.4:

Premise one: It is probably the case that Marianne is wearing jeans

Premise two: If it is not the case that Marianne is wearing jeans then it is not the case that it is Friday

Conclusion: It is probably the case that it is not Friday.

We can't formalise argument 7.4. This is because its validity depends on the meaning of 'probably'. The validity of argument 7.3 doesn't, so it *can* be formalised:

Interpretation:

   P: It is probably the case that Marianne is wearing jeans

   Q: It is Friday

   Premise one: P

   Premise two: (If P then Q)

   Conclusion: Q.

Ability Three: Symbols for Truth Functional

Connectives

In order fully to formalise English sentences as wffs (well-formed formulae) of PL, we will use symbols representing the truth-functional connectives of PL.

There are five such connectives. Here they are, together with the symbols used for them and the nearest English translation:

Truth-functional connective	Symbol	English Translation
Negation	~	It is not the case that
Conjunction	&	And
Disjunction	v	Or
Conditional	→	If/then
Biconditional	↔	If and only if

There are 'notational variants' for each of these symbols. Here are a few of them:

~P	P & Q	P ∨ Q	P → Q	P ↔ Q
¬P	P ∧ Q			P ≡ Q
-P	P • Q	P + Q	P ⊃ Q	P iff Q
P	PQ			

Truth-table Definitions

Each truth-functional connective is defined by its truth-table, as follows:

Negation:

P	~P
T	F
F	T

The truth-table definition of tells us that whenever P is true, the negation of P is false and vice versa.

Conjunction

P	Q	(P & Q)
T	T	T
T	F	F
F	T	F
F	F	F

The truth-table for conjunction tells us that that the ampersand (P & Q) is true only when both its conjuncts are true. Otherwise it is false.

Disjunction

P	Q	(P v Q)
T	T	T
T	F	T
F	T	T
F	F	F

The truth-table for disjunction tells us that (P V Q) is true in every world except that in which both disjuncts are false. Remember that in PL 'or' is used in the inclusive sense, not in the exclusive sense of only one or the other being true.

Conditional

P	Q	(P → Q)
T	T	T
T	F	F
F	T	T
F	F	T

The truth-table for the conditional tells us that (P → Q) is false only if P is true and Q is false. Otherwise it is true. This is counterintuitive and we'll discuss it below.

Biconditional

P	Q	(P ↔ Q)
T	T	T
T	F	F
F	T	F
F	F	T

The truth-table for the biconditional tells us that (P ↔ Q) is true when both the sentence letters flanking the biconditional are true, or when both these sentence letters are false. If the two sentence letters differ in truth value the biconditional is false.

I will often put all these definitions together in one truth-table – this saves time, effort and space!

Here is the result:

P	Q	~P	(P & Q)	(P v Q)	(P→Q)	(P↔Q)
T	T	F	T	T	T	T
T	F		F	T	F	F
F	T	T	F	T	T	F
F	F		F	F	T	T

The entry for negation looks a bit odd but this is because being a unary truth functor it doesn't need values for *two* sentence letters, but only for one.

Let's now look at the pitfalls of translating English sentences with these operators.

Negation: The 'Tilde'

The formula '~ P' means 'it is not the case that P'. So if 'P' is 'Marianne is wearing jeans', '~ P' is 'it is not the case that Marianne is wearing jeans'. We call '~' the 'tilde', which is pronounced 'tilda'.

Importantly '~ P' does *not* mean just 'Marianne is *not* wearing jeans'. PL does not enable us to look *inside* a sentence. It cannot, therefore, distinguish between 'Marianne is not wearing jeans' and 'it is not the case that Marianne is wearing jeans'.

The tilde cancels *all* the implications of 'Marianne is wearing jeans' including the implication that Marianne *exists*. 'It is not the case that Marianne is wearing jeans' will be true just in case 'Marianne is wearing jeans' is false, whatever the reason for that sentence's being false.

You might reasonably ask whether you should use the tilde to translate an English sentence such as:

6)   Marianne is not wearing jeans

As '~' cancels all implications, to translate 'Marianne is not wearing jeans' as '~ P' is to imply not just that Marianne is not wearing jeans (which is all the English sentence means), but also that Marianne might not exist.

Even so, the tilde usually is used to translate 'Marianne is not wearing jeans'. It is the nearest we can get to the English in the language of PL.

All the following sentences can be translated with the negation operator:

1.   Jane is not coming (~ Jane is coming)

2.   There's no chance he will win (~ he will win)

3.   It isn't as if she needs a job (~ she needs a job)

4.   He didn't want the picture (~ he wanted the picture)

5.   Jim never went to work (~ Jim went to work)

None of these is a perfect translation of the English. In 5 we lose the implication that there is *no* occasion on which he went to work, rather than that he simply didn't go to work today (or whenever).

In 2 we lose the emphasis of 'there's no chance'. These infelicities mean that our translations are far from perfect.

Nevertheless, these translations are the nearest we are going to get.

This exercise will help consolidate your understanding of negation.

Exercise 7.6: Translate the following sentences as negations, drawing attention to infelicities in translation

1. Children won't be allowed

2. I have stopped beating my dog

3. She didn't perform well

4. Pegasus does not exist

5. There was no-one home

6. He'll never get in

Answers on page 387

Conjunction

I introduced 'and' as truth-functional above. But in English the use of 'and' can be complicated.

If an English 'and' connects two predicates as in 'the cat is black and white' you should not use the ampersand of conjunction (&). 'The cat is black and white' does *not* mean 'the cat is black *and* the cat is white'. You should use the conjunction only when 'and' connects two free standing *sentences.*

Another pitfall you will meet with 'and' is with sentences like the following:

7)   Philosophers who drink are boring

8)   Philosophers, who drink, are boring

Only one of these sentences can be translated by means of the truth-functional connective '&'. Can you say which one?

If you said sentence 8) you'd be right. Sentence 8) says, of *all* philosophers, both that they drink *and* that they are boring. The underlying grammar tells us that this is, therefore, a conjunction:

9)   (Philosophers drink & philosophers are boring)

Sentence 7), however, is a simple sentence. It says, of *philosophers who drink*, that they are boring. Philosophers who don't drink have been excluded from the discussion.

Here are some of the numerous ways in which conjunction manifests itself in English:

1.   The journey was comfortable *if* slow (The journey was comfortable & the journey was slow)

2.   *Although* the car was old it ran well (the car was old & the car ran well)

3.   She was poor *but* beautiful (she was poor & she was beautiful)

4.   *Neither* I *nor* James will get the job (I will not get the job & James will not get the job)

5. The teabags are in the canister, *which* is on the second shelf (the canister is on the second shelf & the teabags are in the canister)

6. The menu offers a choice between salmon or steak (the menu offers salmon & the menu offers steak)

Again some translations are infelicitous. In 2 and 3 we lose the implication there is something unusual about a car's being old but running well, and about someone's being poor *and* beautiful.

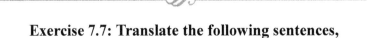

Exercise 7.7: Translate the following sentences, where possible, as conjunctions, drawing attention to infelicities in translation.

If the conjunction can't be used say why.

1. Jane was happy but exhausted

2. Although the tick was there it was faint

3. Jim and Jules were twins

4. The student who was looking tired was reading

5. The book, which was the course text book, was a very long one

6. Your suggestion is both incorrect and outrageous.

7. Headington and Cumnor are both suburbs of Oxford

8. Headington and Cumnor are five miles apart

Answers on page 388

Disjunction

The English 'or' is translated by means of the disjunction sign. This is the sign: 'V', usually called 'vel', pronounced exactly as it is read. The English 'or' can be either inclusive or exclusive. So if I say 'You can have apple pie or ice cream', I might mean that you can have either apple pie, or ice cream, or *both*, or that you can have either apple pie or ice cream but *not* both.

In the first case my 'or' is inclusive. In the second case it is exclusive.

Unlike the English 'or' the 'V' of PL is *always* inclusive. This means that if either of the two disjuncts are true, the formula is always true. The truth-table definition for vel makes this clear.

This doesn't mean we can't, in the language of PL capture an exclusive 'or'. To do so we combine vel with a conjunction and a negation:

10) ((You can have apple pie V you can have ice cream) **&** ~ (you can have apple pie **&** you can have ice cream))

Here are some sentences that can be translated by means of the vel:

1. *Unless* the Board is sacked, the company will deteriorate (the Board is sacked V the company will deteriorate)

2. He is a genius *or* a hypocrite (he is a genius V he is a hypocrite)

3. *Unless* you wear a seat belt you will be injured (you will wear a seat belt V you will be injured)

4. Either the phone will work or it won't (the phone will work ∨ it's not the case the phone will work)

Exercise 7.8: Translate the following sentences by means of the vel

1. James is coming with Anna unless he is late.

2. We must impose austerity or we'll never reduce the national debt.

3. We'll go to the festival unless the weather is foul.

4. Either Jane is coming, or John will opt out.

Answers on page 389

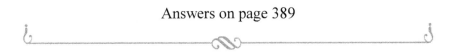

Conditional

The truth-functional conditional most unlike its English counterpart is the conditional: 'if...then', which is formalised as '→', usually called 'arrow'.

Here is the truth-table definition for the conditional:

P	Q	(P→Q)
T	T	T
T	F	F
F	T	T
F	F	T

You will note that the conditional is false *only* if its antecedent (the sentence in the 'if' position) is true *and* its consequent (the sentence in the 'then' position) is false. Otherwise the conditional is true. In particular the conditional is always true if its antecedent is false, or if its consequent is true.

This seems very odd to most English speakers. If we take a sentence such as 'If it rains you'll get wet', we *wouldn't* usually say that its truth is guaranteed by the falsehood of 'it's raining' or by the truth of 'you'll get wet'. Yet, the conditional of PL is such that any sentence translated as $(P \rightarrow Q)$ *will* be true under these conditions.

The oddness of this is slightly reduced by the recognition that the truth-table for $(P \rightarrow Q)$ gives it the same truth conditions as 'it's not the case that P *and* not-Q'; i.e. $\sim (P \And \sim Q)$.

It is intuitively right, isn't it, that if we say 'if it rains you will get wet' we are saying 'it is not the case that it will rain and you *won't* get wet'. We are implying, in other words, a connection between its raining, and your getting wet, that makes the former sufficient for the latter.

Stand-Alone Sentences

In the last chapter I claimed that we couldn't strip the content from the counterexample set of argument 5.13 in the way we had stripped it from the counterexample set of argument 5.12. I promised, in this chapter, to explain why not.

We have already seen one problem: the validity of argument 5.13 turns on its predicate structure and not solely on its propositional structure. But there is another problem, this time to do with premise one.

Here again is premise one:

11) If the premises of argument 5.11 are true, then the conclusion of argument 5.11 must be true.

Ask yourself whether the antecedent and the consequent of this conditional stand alone with respect to meaning? Or whether it is the case that we can only understand one in the context of the other?

Sometimes it is possible to understand the consequent of a conditional *only* in the light of its antecedent. For example if I say 'If I drop the vase it will break', the consequent ('it will break') makes sense only in the context of the antecedent ('I drop the vase'). After all why should the vase break if I *don't* drop it?

Sentence connectives connect sentences that stand alone . If we cannot separate the sentences whilst preserving their meaning, then we can't use a sentence connective.

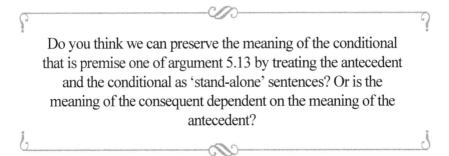

Do you think we can preserve the meaning of the conditional that is premise one of argument 5.13 by treating the antecedent and the conditional as 'stand-alone' sentences? Or is the meaning of the consequent dependent on the meaning of the antecedent?

It is a subtle point, but consider this. If we take the consequent of this conditional and treat it as a stand-alone sentence we get:

12) The conclusion of argument 5.11 must be true.

But this implies that the conclusion of argument 5.11 is *a tautology*, that it is *necessarily true*.

But this is not an implication of the sentence we are trying to formalise is it? That sentence says only that the conclusion of argument 5.11 is necessarily true *in the context of the truth of the premises of argument 5.11*.

The only way to represent the actual meaning of the first sentence of the counterexample set of argument 5.13 is by means of a single sentence letter:

P: If the premises of argument 5.11 are true then the
     conclusion of argument 5.11 must be true.

The constituent sentences of this conditional are not free-standing.

We can only formalise sentences in the language of PL if they are *free-standing* sentences . If their meaning depends on the meaning of any other sentence, we lose this part of the meaning in formalising them by means of sentence connectives.

In the case of sentence 11) we lose *too much* meaning if we use the arrow.

You might reasonably ask 'how do I tell when the meaning I lose in translation is *too much* meaning to lose'? There is no easy answer to this question. It is a judgment call. I can only promise that as you gain experience it will get easier (mainly because you'll start to see the difficulties for yourself).

Even If

You might think that a sentence like 'even if it is raining, you won't get wet' would be translated by the conditional. But this is wrong. This sentence means simply 'you won't get wet'. The 'even if' cancels itself out, and is used only for emphasis.

Only if

People are often thrown by the addition of the word 'only' to a conditional sentence. Consider the difference between:

13) If it is raining you'll get wet.

14) You'll only get wet if it rains.

Sentence 13) claims that it is a *sufficient* condition of your getting wet that it is raining.

This sentence does not say that its raining is a *necessary* condition of your getting wet. It is consistent with this sentence that you could get wet even if it isn't raining.

Sentence 14), on the other hand, claims that the rain is a *necessary* condition of your getting wet. It is not consistent with this sentence that you could get wet even if it isn't raining.

PL captures this by reversing the direction of the arrow.

15) (it is raining → you get wet)

This formalises sentence 13) and tells us that the fact it is raining is *sufficient* for your getting wet, allowing for the possibility that you might get wet by other means.

16) (You get wet → it is raining)

This formalises sentence 14) and tells us that its raining is a *necessary* condition of your getting wet (i.e. that if you are wet it is raining)

Be very careful, when translating, to get the right impact of 'only'. In particular beware of confusing an 'only if' with an 'if and only if'. The latter is properly formalised only with the biconditional.

Here are some sentences that can be translated with the conditional:

1. If your extremities are turning blue, you are too cold. (Your extremities are turning blue → you are too cold)

2. The postman will only deliver if it is Friday. (if the postman is delivering → it is Friday)

3. You are more likely to have an accident if you don't wear your seatbelt. (you don't wear your seatbelt → you are more likely to have an accident)

4. If you get a pension you can't get carers' allowance. (you get a pension → you can't get carers' allowance)

5. Your child can be enrolled in school only if he is nearly 5 years old. (your child can be enrolled in school → your child is nearly five)

6. If you broke the law you will be punished. (you broke the law → you will be punished)

Exercise 7.9: Translate the following sentences by means of the arrow drawing attention to any infelicities in translation:

1. Assuming he has trained properly, he should win.

2. If one more student fails to hand in their work, I'll explode.

3. The paper will only turn red if the liquid is acidic.

4. If the sun is out let's have a picnic.

5. Supposing he is right, then I will get the sack.

Answers on page 389

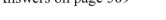

Biconditional

The biconditional is used for the English phrase 'if and only if'. It alerts us to the fact that two sentences are true and false under precisely the same conditions. The truth of each sentence is both necessary and sufficient for the truth of the other.

We should use the biconditional *only* when a conditional *runs in both directions*. Very importantly you should not, as so many of my undergraduates do, reach for the biconditional every time you see an 'only'. In the case of the biconditional we do not have simply a necessary condition, or simply a sufficient condition, we have conditions *both* necessary *and* sufficient.

Take this sentence:

17) You can vote if and only if you are on the electoral roll.

This tells us that being on the electoral role is both necessary and sufficient for being able to vote. So if you are on the electoral roll, you can vote. And if you can vote, you are on the electoral roll. Both of the following, therefore, are true:

18) (You are on the electoral roll → you can vote)

19) (You can vote → you are on the electoral roll)

If only one of these is true you *must not* use the biconditional. Do not use a biconditional unless you are sure the arrow runs in both directions.

Here are some sentences that can be translated by means of the biconditional:

1. The number is even if and only if it is divisible by two (the number is even ↔ the number is divisible by two)

2. He is a bachelor just in case he is an unmarried adult male ('just in case' is an American expression that means 'iff) (he is a bachelor ↔ he is an unmarried adult male)

3. You can join the library if and only if you are a local resident (you can join the library ↔ you are a local resident)

Please go over each of these examples and check that you are certain what I mean about the arrow's *running each way*.

Exercise 7.10: Translate the following sentences by means of the biconditional drawing attention to any infelicities in translation

1. You can enter the competition if, and only if, you are eligible.

2. It is a necessary and a sufficient condition of his becoming a doctor that his thesis passes.

3. Whoever slays the dragon will marry the princess.

Answers on page 390

Before we turn to the final ability we'll discuss, let's test our ability to formalise English sentences into the language of PL:

Exercise 7.11: Using the truth functor symbols of PL and the interpretation provided, please translate the premises and conclusion of the target argument into the language of PL

Interpretation:

P: The economy is flourishing

Q: Herr Kohl is humiliated

R: Herr Kohl will get grass roots support

S: The German Government will last

Premise one: The economy is not flourishing

Premise two: Herr Kohl is humiliated

Premise three: Herr Kohl will not get grass roots support if Herr Kohl is humiliated

Premise four: Unless Herr Kohl gets grass roots support, the German Government will only last if the economy flourishes

Conclusion: The German Government won't last.

Answers on page 390

Ability Four: Representing Argument Claims as Sequents of PL

To put forward an argument is to claim that the conclusion of that argument *follows from* its premises. An argument is *not* just a set of sentences.

We have not fully formalised an English argument , therefore, until we have formalised the argument claim; until we have said *which* sentence is playing the role of the conclusion, and which sentences the role of the premises.

We do this with sequents. There are two types of sequent, *semantic* sequents, and *syntactic* sequents. When we use the latter we formalise at an even deeper level than we do when we use the former. Let's start, therefore, by discussing semantic sequents.

Argument Claims

In chapter two we analysed the target argument:

"Even though there is no opposition, the economy is going to the dogs and Herr Kohl is about to be humiliated by his EC partners. Certainly, if the economy flourishes, his Government will survive. But grass roots support will inevitably fade if Herr Kohl is humiliated, and unless he gets that support, his Government will only last in a flourishing economy."

In this chapter we took that analysis, and formalised the constituent sentences of the argument in accordance with this interpretation:

P: The economy is flourishing

Q: Herr Kohl is humiliated

R: Herr Kohl will get grass roots support

S: The German Government will last

This has given us:

Premise one: $\sim P$

Premise two: Q

Premise three: $(Q \rightarrow \sim R)$

Premise four: $(R \vee (S \rightarrow P))$

Conclusion: $\sim S.$

As yet, though, we haven't formalised *the argument claim.* At the moment we are still using English words, and the logic-book layout, to indicate the claim being made by the one using the argument.

Semantic Sequents

The sequents allows us to formalise the argument claim itself. The first sequent we'll look at is the semantic sequent, which is symbolised: '$\vDash$'. This symbol is often called the 'semantic turnstile'.

This symbol means:

Def: *Semantic sequent* ($\models$)**: There is no structure in which the formulae on the left hand side are true and the formula on the right hand side false.**

This formalises the argument by putting the wffs that are premises on the left hand side of the sequent and the wff that is the conclusion on the right hand side of the sequent.

Here is the sequent that formalises the argument above:

20) $\sim P, Q, (Q \rightarrow \sim R), (R \vee (S \rightarrow P)) \models \sim S$

Notice that commas separate the premises, and the sequent is laid out *along* the page. The sequent itself tells us which wffs are the premises (those on the left hand side) and which the conclusion (that on the right).

Semantic sequents are tested by truth-tables. The 'structures' referred to in the definition of a semantic sequent are the rows of the truth-table. In the next chapter we shall be learning how to test them.

But first now let's learn the final step in formalising an argument.

Eliminating Truth Talk

The semantic sequent, because it is tested with truth-tables, still relies on an uninterpreted notion of truth. In order fully to formalise the argument claim we need to eliminate this.

Syntactic Sequents

We do this by means of a syntactic sequent: ' $\vdash$ ' (the syntactic turnstile). Syntactic sequents represent a deeper level of formalisation. If a semantic sequent is correct its corresponding syntactic sequent is correct (and vice versa). We learn about syntactic sequents because they are tested by means of syntactic tableaux and, as you'll see in the next chapter, these are *much* simpler than truth tables.

The syntactic sequent formalises an argument in exactly the same way the semantic sequent does. Our argument therefore becomes:

21) $\sim$ P, Q, (Q $\rightarrow$ $\sim$ R), (R $\vee$ (S $\rightarrow$ P)) $\vdash$ $\sim$ S

Note the replacement of ' $\vDash$ ' with ' $\vdash$ '.

The difference between the two sequents is the way they are understood. With the syntactic sequent we do not mention 'structures', 'truth' or 'falsehood'; in other words even *these* notions are formalised.

This is how we understand the syntactic sequent:

> **Def:** *Syntactic Sequent* ($\vdash$): **The tableaux generated from the counterexample set of this sequent will close.**

The definition of the syntactic sequent will become more intelligible in the next chapter. There we will create counterexample sets from syntactic sequents and generate tableaux from them. We will then evaluate these arguments claims by seeing whether or not these tableaux close.

Tautologies and Contradictions

Sometimes we want to claim a set of formulae are contradictory (such that it is logically impossible for them to be true together), or that they are tautologous (such that they are true in every possible world).

Both claims can be captured by means of sequents as follows.

$$\models (P \lor \sim P)$$

This sequent states that there is no structure in which $(P \lor \sim P)$ is false (in other words that $(P \lor \sim P)$ is a tautology). If you do the truth table for it you will find that it is true in each structure.

Whilst this one:

$$(P \,\&\, \sim P) \models$$

states that there is no structure in which $(P \,\&\, \sim P)$ is true (in other words that $(P \,\&\, \sim P)$ is a contradiction). If you generate a truth table from it you will find that it is false in each structure.

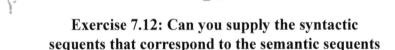

Exercise 7.12: Can you supply the syntactic sequents that correspond to the semantic sequents above, and explain their meaning?

Answers on page 391

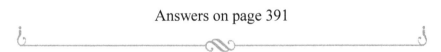

We have now finished learning how to represent English arguments as sequents of PL. It remains only for you to check you can:

- recognise those arguments to which PL applies;

- use the truth-table test to identify truth-functional sentence connectives;

- explain the truth-table definitions of all the truth functors of PL;

- explain why truth-tables represent meanings;

- make use of brackets to indicate the scope of truth functional connectives;

- translate English sentences into wffs (well-formed formulae of PL);

- avoid the pitfalls of translating English sentences into wffs;

- formalise English argument claims into semantic and syntactic sequents;

- explain the meaning of such sequents.

I hope that you feel you can do these things. If not, re-read the appropriate section, before turning to the next chapter.

Well done for finishing this chapter. Quite a slog! Congratulations.

I really mean this: this chapter is *far* harder than anything you have done in the book so far and you really have done well to finish it.

Let's end with a quick quiz.

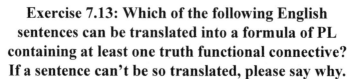

Exercise 7.13: Which of the following English sentences can be translated into a formula of PL containing at least one truth functional connective? If a sentence can't be so translated, please say why. If it can be translated, please translate it.

1. I know that Marianne is wearing jeans

2. Marianne is not wearing jeans

3. Marianne is wearing jeans or it is Friday

4. It is hard to say whether Marianne is wearing jeans

5. If Marianne is wearing jeans then it is Friday

Answers on page 392

CHAPTER EIGHT

The Rules of Propositional Logic

This chapter corresponds to the podcasts three and four in the series: A Romp Through the Foothills of Logic. This is available only in audio and you'll find it at metafore.com/ CR8audio1 and metafore.com/CR8audio2 You will also find the short video podcasts 'Testing Semantic Sequents' (at metafore.com/ CRTestingSemanticSequents) and 'Testing Syntactic Sequents' (at metafore.com/CRTestingSyntacticSequents) useful. The transcripts are at http://mariannetalbot.co.uk/transcripts.

I really recommend watching the podcasts for this chapter. It will make learning to apply the rules a great deal easier.

In this chapter you will learn the rules of propositional logic (henceforth PL). This will enable you mechanically to evaluate any deductive argument that can be formalised as a sequent of PL. It is so easy to apply the rules that even computers can do it.

A careful reading of this chapter will ensure you'll be able to:

- construct truth tables by which to identify the truth conditions of wffs;

- explain how truth tables work;

- understand how syntactic tableaux correspond to truth table definitions;

- test semantic sequents by means of truth tables;

- test syntactic sequents by means of tableaux;

- understand the impact of a syntactic sequent's being open or closed;

- identify the counterexample for any incorrect sequent.

As usual we'll check you can do all this at the end of the chapter.

Evaluating an Argument by Means of Propositional Logic

In the last chapter we looked at the steps needed to translate an English argument into a sequent of PL. We learned that we might formalise the argument as a *semantic sequent*, or that we might go one step deeper and formalise it as a *syntactic sequent.*

In this chapter we shall be learning the steps needed to evaluate these sequents. This means we'll learn how to:

(a) use truth tables to demonstrate the truth or falsehood of an argument claim formalised as a semantic sequent;

(b) use syntactic tableaux to demonstrate the truth or falsehood of an argument claim formalised as a syntactic sequent.

Using Truth Tables to Evaluate Semantic Sequents

In chapter six we saw that the truth table definition of the conditional or 'arrow' seems odd to an English speaker. I explained it by saying that the truth table for $(P \rightarrow Q)$ is the *same* as that for 'it is not the case P and not-Q' or $\sim (P \mathbin{\&} \sim Q)$.

We are going to start this chapter by demonstrating this. The skills we need to do it are the very skills we need to apply the rules of PL to a semantic sequent.

Here is the truth table for the conditional:

P	Q	(P→Q)
T	T	T
T	F	F
F	T	T
F	F	T

This is for the purpose of comparison. Our intention is now to complete the truth table for ~ (P & ~ Q), to see that they really are the same.

P	Q	~P	(P & Q)
T	T	F	T
T	F		F
F	T	T	F
F	F		F

The truth table definitions for the conjunction and negation operators will be needed to complete this truth table. You might want to make a note of them so you can refer to them during our discussion. Here they are put together in one truth table (note the negation looks odd again – we met this in chapter six: being a unary connective it only needs two truth values, not four):

Starting Off: The Empty Truth Table

Here is an empty truth table, showing only the formula for which we were constructing a truth table, and the four possible combinations of truth value for the two sentence letters:

P	Q	~(P & ~Q)
T	T	
T	F	
F	T	
F	F	

Let's start by making sure we can identify each row and each column, so we can follow each step easily:

	P	Q	~(P & ~Q)
1	T	T	
2	T	F	
3	F	T	
4	F	F	
	1	2	3 4 5 6 7

You might like to copy this blank truth table so you can complete the steps as (or even before!) I do.

Rows and Possible Situations

Each numbered row represents a possible situation. Row 1 is the situation in which 'P' is true *and* 'Q' is true. Row 2 is the situation in which 'P' is true and 'Q' is false, and so on.

There are only four possible situations because there are only four possible combinations of truth values. This is because there are two sentence letters and each sentence letter, bivalence tells us, has one of only two possible truth values.

If you had a truth table with three sentence letters then, given that each would have one of the only two possible truth values, there would be 8 possible situations, as shown here (with a change of formula to add the extra sentence letter):

R	P	Q	~(P & ~(Q ∨ R))
T	T	T	
T	T	F	
T	F	T	
T	F	F	
F	T	T	
F	T	F	
F	F	T	
F	F	F	

If you had a truth table with four sentence letters then there would be sixteen possible situations and so on. When completing the 'key' for a truth table, you always put 'true' and 'false' on alternate rows in the column for the most right hand sentence letter, then 2 'true's and two 'false's alternately in the next most right hand column, then 4 'true's and four 'false's, then 8.....

I think you can see why, as you multiply the sentence letters, truth tables become quite wearisome. You will be glad of syntactic tableaux by the time we get to them.

Let's now work through each step of the completion of this numbered truth table.

Step One: The Sentence Letters

When we are learning how to complete a truth table the first step involves filling in, in each row, under each sentence letter, the truth value given for that letter in that row. This couldn't be simpler. All we need to do is copy the letters from columns 1 and 2 into columns 4 and 7, making them lower case as we do so.

	P	Q	~(P & ~ Q)	
1	T	T	t	t
2	T	F	t	f
3	F	T	f	t
4	F	F	f	f
	1	2	3 4 5	6 7

These letters are lower case to show that they are only a step along the way. When we finally get to the truth value for the wff as a whole we will make them upper case and underline them. This will distinguish them from all the other truth values cluttering up the table.

When you are adept at truth tables you won't have to insert truth values for the sentence letters. You'll be able simply to read them off from the 'key'. Your truth tables will then be less cluttered. For now, though, adding these truth values will help you avoid silly mistakes. (It won't *ensure* you avoid silly mistakes – this is one of the problems with truth tables: it is very easy to make silly mistakes. Don't beat yourself up though – we all do it!).

Step Two: The Truth-Functional Connective with the Smallest Scope

Next we work out which truth-functional connective has the smallest scope. The 'scope' of an operator consists in the sentence letters and other connectives on which it operates. The negation operator in column 6 of the truth table below does not, for example, operate on the conjunction operator. Its scope is *only* the sentence letter 'Q'. The scope of the negation operator in column 3, on the other hand, is the whole formula.

To work out which truth functional connective has the smallest scope we identify each truth-functional connective in the wff, determine its scope, then focus on the operator with the smallest one.

	P	Q	~(P & ~ Q)	
1	T	T	t	t
2	T	F	t	f
3	F	T	f	t
4	F	F	f	f
	1	2	3 4 5	6 7

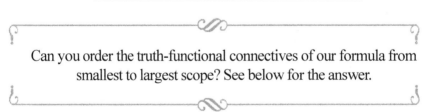

Can you order the truth-functional connectives of our formula from smallest to largest scope? See below for the answer.

There are three truth-functional connectives in this formula; two negation signs (one in column 3, the other in column 6) and one conjunction (in column 5).

The scope of the negation sign in column 6 is, as we have seen, simply the 'Q' in column 7. The scope of the conjunction in column 5 is everything from the 'P' in column 4, to the 'Q' in column 7 (so everything within the brackets). The scope of the negation sign outside the brackets (the one in column 3) is the whole bracketed formula.

It is, therefore, the negation sign in column 6 that has the smallest scope. The truth-functional connective with the next smallest scope is the conjunction in column 5. The truth-functional connective with the largest scope is the negation in column 3.

Once we have identified the operator with the smallest scope we provide truth values for it. In this we are guided by the truth table definition for the operator, in this case negation.

The negation operator reverses the truth value of 'Q' (i.e. the truth values in column 7). So wherever there is a 't' in column 7 we put an 'f' in column 6, and wherever there is an 'f' in column 7 we put a 't' in column 6.

Here is the truth table with this step added:

	P	Q	~(P & ~ Q)		
1	T	T	t	f	t
2	T	F	t	t	f
3	F	T	f	f	t
4	F	F	f	t	f
	1	2	3 4 5	6 7	

We have again used lower case letters for the truth values because upper case letters will be used only for the final step: the truth value we are really concerned with.

From this point on we shall be ignoring the truth values in column 7, because it is the truth values in column 6 that matter in calculating the truth value of the whole formula. If you like you can emphasise this by crossing through the truth values we shan't be needing any more.

Step Three: The Operator With the Next Smallest Scope

We now turn to the operator with the next smallest scope; the conjunction in column 5.

Using the truth table definition of '&' and the truth values of the formula flanking the conjunction (the truth values under 'P' in column 4, and the truth values under the negation in column 6) we work out the truth values of the conjunction noting them in column 5. Here is the result of this step:

	P	Q	~(P & ~ Q)
1	T	T	t f f t
2	T	F	t t t f
3	F	T	f f f t
4	F	F	f f t f
	1	2	3 4 5 6 7

From now on it is only the truth values in column 5 that matter. The truth values in column 5 are those for the whole of the formula inside the brackets. It is *these* that are negated by the negation operator outside the brackets.

302

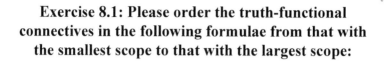

Exercise 8.1: Please order the truth-functional connectives in the following formulae from that with the smallest scope to that with the largest scope:

1. $(P \rightarrow \sim Q)$

2. $\sim(P \lor Q)$

3. $(P \lor \sim Q)$

4. $(R \rightarrow (P \ \& \sim Q))$

5. $((P \lor R) \leftrightarrow Q)$

Answers on page 393

Step Four: The Operator With the Largest Scope

Finally we get to the last operator, the truth functional connective with the largest scope. This is the negation in column 3. This is the column that matters to us, because this truth value is the truth value of the wff as a whole. The truth values in column 3, taken together, give us the truth *conditions* of this wff.

Can you say why a completed truth table represents the truth conditions of a wff?

The truth table represents every possible combination of truth values of each of the constituent sentences of a wff. This enables us to determine the truth value of the whole wff in every possible situation. To be able to determine this is to grasp the truth *conditions* (or weak meaning) of the wff.

We generate this set of truth values by again using the truth table definition of the negation sign. This time, the negation is operating on the truth value of the conjunction sign in column 5. As always the negation sign reverses the truth value. So if the conjunction is true (if there is a 't' in column 5), the negation of the conjunction is false (and you should put an 'f' in column 3). Here is the result of this step:

	P	Q	~(P & ~ Q)
1	T	T	<u>T</u> t f f t
2	T	F	<u>F</u> t t t f
3	F	T	<u>T</u> f f f t
4	F	F	<u>T</u> f f t f
	1	2	3 4 5 6 7

This time I have put the truth values in bold upper case letters and underlined them. This emphasises that they tell us the truth value of the whole formula. Together they represent the truth conditions – the weak meaning - of the whole wff.

Our truth table is now complete. We now know that our wff is true in every situation *except* the situation in which 'P' is true and 'Q' false (which makes sense doesn't it?). We can also see that it has precisely the same truth table as the arrow (check this out with the truth-table definition of the arrow on page 269). I trust that makes you feel slightly better about the oddness of the truth table definition of the arrow?

I hope that you now feel you know exactly how to construct truth tables even if you will (of course) need more practice before you can be entirely confident. Now you can construct complex truth tables you can also evaluate semantic sequents. So you've learned a lot already.

Exercise 8.2: Please provide complete truth tables for the following wffs, indicating which column gives us the truth value for the whole wff by using upper case, underlined, truth values.

1. $(P \rightarrow \sim Q)$

2. $\sim (P \vee Q)$

3. $(P \vee \sim Q)$

4. $(R \rightarrow (P \& \sim Q))$

5. $((P \vee R) \leftrightarrow Q)$

To complete this quiz you will need all the truth table definitions. Here they are (as usual all in one table to save space):

P	Q	~P	(P & Q)	(P v Q)	(P→Q)	(P↔Q)
T	T	F	T	T	T	T
T	F		F	T	F	F
F	T	T	F	T	T	F
F	F		F	F	T	T

Answers on page 394

From Formulae to Argument Claims

Now let's use a truth table to evaluate a sequent. This involves completing the truth table for all the formulae of the sequent, *and* for the sequent itself.

A sequent is the formalisation of an argument claim. An argument claim is a claim to the effect that the conclusion follows from the premises. *This* is the claim we are testing. We want to know whether it is indeed the case that there is no logically possible situation in which the premises are true yet the conclusion false.

Let's start learning how to test sequents with a very easy one:

1) $(P \& Q) \models \sim Q$

This reads:

> **there is no structure in which all the formulae on the left hand side (henceforth LHS) of $\models$ are true and the formulae on the right hand side (henceforth RHS) of $\models$ false.**

This sequent is incorrect. ~Q does *not* follow from (P & Q). On the contrary, if (P & Q) is true then Q *must* be true.

If the sequent is incorrect we know that there should be at least one logically possible situation (one row of the truth table) in which the formula on the LHS of the sequent is true and that on the RHS false.

Let's see how to construct the truth table that will show this.

Step One: The Blank Truth Table

First we identify the number of sentence letters and draw a blank truth table with the appropriate number of rows:

P	Q	(P & Q) $\models$ ~Q
T	T	
T	F	
F	T	
F	F	

You will note that where, in the truth table above, we had a single formula, we now have a whole sequent consisting of two formulae, and the sequent itself.

As before, let's add numbers to the rows and columns to make our discussion easier.

	P	Q	(P & Q) $\models$ ~ Q
1	T	T	
2	T	F	
3	F	T	
4	F	F	
	1	2	3 4 5 6 7 8

Our final aim, in testing a sequent is to decide whether the sequent itself (row 6) is correct. We could signify this by means of a truth value in column 6 (T= it is correct, F= it isn't correct), but I prefer to distinguish sequents from formulae by using:

- a tick for correct (the situation in which the premises are all true and the conclusion also true);

- a cross for incorrect (the situation in which the premises are all true and the conclusion false).

We always look for crosses first, of course, because if there is even one cross, this suffices to show that the whole sequent is incorrect. As we complete the truth table you can, if you like, complete lower case truth values under the sentence letters. Preferring an uncluttered truth table, I am not going to do this. Instead I will complete the truth value only for the connectives.

Step Two: The Easiest Formula

In testing a semantic sequent we nearly always have to provide truth values for two or more formulae. The only time this isn't the case is when we are testing the claim that a formula is a tautology or a contradiction. Then it is possible that there will be only one formula to the right or to the left of the sequent.

Here are the two examples we used in chapter seven (page 290) to illustrate this:

$$\models (P \lor \sim P)$$

If you check the definition of the sequent you will see that this states that there is no structure in which $(P \lor \sim P)$ is false. It doesn't mention the LHS because there is no formula on the LHS. This sequent states that $(P \lor \sim P)$ is a tautology. If you do the truth table for it you will find that it is true in each structure.

The sequent below states that there is no structure in which (P & ~ P) is true. It doesn't mention the formula on the RHS because there isn't one.

(P & ~ P) ⊨

This sequent states that (P & ~ P) is a contradiction. If you generate a truth table from it you will find that it is false in each structure.

In the normal case (i.e. when we are not testing tautologies or contradictions) we must choose which formula we should do first. It doesn't matter which you choose. I am going to start with the easiest formula.

For our sequent the easiest formula is the '~ Q' in columns 7 and 8. The connective (in column 7) is a negation sign, and it therefore reverses the truth value of 'Q'. The truth value of 'Q' is shown in column 2 (and would appear in column 8 if we were adding truth values for sentence letters). Here is the result:

	P	Q	(P & Q) ⊨ ~ Q
1	T	T	F
2	T	F	T
3	F	T	F
4	F	F	T
	1	2	3 4 5 6 7 8

When we were calculating the truth value of a single formula the only truth value underlined and in upper case letters was the final one. In testing a sequent we are calculating the truth value of more than one formula and a sequent.

It is best to use underlined capital letters for each whole formula (and lower case letters for the sub-formulae). It is from the capital letters that we calculate whether the sequent itself is correct.

Step Three: The Hardest Formula

Because our sequent is such a simple one, we have only one formula left; the one on the left hand side. This is a simple conjunction. All we need to add is the appropriate truth values as guided by the truth table definition of '&'.

If you are calculating the truth value of the conjunction without adding the lower case truth values for the sentence letters flanking it, make sure you definitely have the right values for the flanking letters. It is very easy to make a mistake here. That it is so easy to make mistakes is not obvious here because the sentence letters you need are the same ones, in the same order, as those in the key. It is not always this easy.

Here is the result of this step:

	P	Q	(P & Q) ⊨ ~ Q	
1	T	T	T̲	F
2	T	F	F̲	T̲
3	F	T	F̲	F
4	F	F	F̲	T̲
	1	2	3 4 5	6 7 8

We can now move on to determining, of the sequent itself, whether or not it is correct.

Step Four: Evaluating the Sequent in Situation 1

We know that an argument is valid if there is no possible situation in which all the premises are true and the conclusion false. We also know that a truth table represents the possible combinations of truth values of every formulae of the sequent in every possible situation. This enables us to see (almost) at a glance, whether the sequent is correct or if there is a counterexample.

We only need *one* situation in which the formula on the LHS is true and that on the RHS false, to demonstrate the incorrectness of the sequent. But it is only the whole truth table that can demonstrate that the sequent is correct in *every* possible situation: i.e. that there is *no* possible situation in which all the premises true and the conclusion false.

	P	Q	(P & Q) ⊨ ~ Q
1	T	T	T x F
2	T	F	F T
3	F	T	F F·
4	F	F	F T
	1	2	3 4 5 6 7 8

In this case the very first situation we look at, row 1, provides us with a counterexample. In row 1 the sole formula on the LHS (the premise) is true, but the formula on the RHS (the conclusion) is false. We can immediately put a cross in row 1, column 6.

We now know immediately not only that *there is* a counterexample, we also what that counterexample is: it is the situation in which 'P' is true *and* 'Q' is true.

All we need now is an interpretation and we will have the counterexample in English.

312

Try using this interpretation to find an argument, and a counterexample;

P: The cat is on the mat
Q: The dog is on the bed

If you can see that the argument claim constructed of this premise and this conclusion is invalid then you have understood! Well done. I hope you also see that the interpretation we provide is irrelevant – *any* argument of this form would be invalid *whatever* its content.

Logic has told us, without any shadow of doubt, that the original argument is invalid. It has also told us in *which* logically possible situation we find a counterexample.

We needn't complete the truth table. One possible situation in which the premises are true, and the conclusion false, is enough. But to complete it we'd just go through all the other rows in the same way, putting a cross if we find another counterexample or a tick if we find a situation in which the formulae on the LHS are true and the formulae on the RHS are also true.

Here is the completed truth table:

	P	Q	(P & Q) ⊨ ~ Q
1	T	T	T̲ x F̲
2	T	F	F̲ - T̲
3	F	T	F̲ - F̲
4	F	F	F̲ - T̲
	1	2	3 4 5 6 7 8

Sadly we don't get to put a tick anywhere in this truth table. There isn't a situation in which the formula on the LHS *and* the formula on the RHS are both true. I leave blank the rows where it is not the case that (all) the formulae on the LHS are true, just to emphasise the fact that we needn't even check the conclusion here – we know that the sequent isn't incorrect just by knowing that it is not the case that all the formulae on the LHS are true.

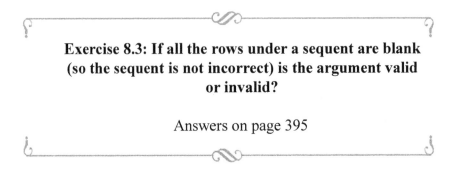

Exercise 8.3: If all the rows under a sequent are blank (so the sequent is not incorrect) is the argument valid or invalid?

Answers on page 395

Even if we had found such a situation, however, it would not have cancelled out the cross in row 1. We only need *one* counterexample to blow a deductive argument out of the water.

Practice your ability to test sequents by means of truth tables with this exercise:

Exercise 8.4: Test the following semantic sequents by means of truth tables, giving counterexamples where possible.

1. (P ∨ Q), P ⊨ (R & Q)

2. (P→Q) ⊨ (P→(Q & R))

3. (P→R), (R→Q) ⊨ (P→R)

4. (P & ~ P) ⊨

5. ⊨ (P ∨ ~ P)

To complete this quiz you will need all the truth table definitions. Here they are together in one table:

P	Q	~P	(P & Q)	(P ∨ Q)	(P→Q)	(P↔Q)
T	T	F	T	T	T	T
T	F		F	T	F	F
F	T	T	F	T	T	F
F	F		F	F	T	T

Answers on page 396

Relating Sequents to Argument Claims

Congratulations! You have now learned how, mechanically, to evaluate English arguments by means of truth tables. This procedure will enable you to show quite conclusively when an argument is or isn't valid (so long as that argument is the right sort of argument to be tested in this way).

It will also enable you to show, again quite conclusively, which counterexamples) to use to demonstrate the invalidity of arguments the premises of which *don't* entail their conclusions. If you have an interpretation, furthermore, you will be able to describe these counterexamples in plain English.

From Semantic Sequents to Syntactic Sequents

But we can formalise an argument to an even deeper level than that of a semantic sequent. At the level of a semantic sequent we are still talking about truth and falsehood, and about logical possibility.

By using syntactic sequents we can even eliminate this. This is desirable to the extent that we are worried about not knowing much *about* truth, falsehood and possibility.

It is also desirable because we can test syntactic sequents with syntactic tableaux. These are *much* easier than truth tables. Like truth tables, though, they will tell us immediately whether our formalised arguments are valid. They will also provide us with counterexamples when these arguments are not valid.

A lot of people find tableaux rather hard. They don't see *how* they work. In fact it isn't so difficult. A tableau is a tree-like representation of the set of sentences that is the counterexample set of an argument. The tableau shows whether these sentences are consistent or inconsistent.

It does this because each time you apply a rule (see below) to a formula, the rule will set out the conditions in which that formula is true. So we start with the complex formula and work through, by applying the rules, to the simple formulae. Each branch (you'll see what I mean by 'branch' below) is an attempt to draw a logically possible situation in which all these formulae are true together (are consistent).

Some branches, though, will represent a *failed* attempt to draw a logically possible situation in which all the formulae of the counterexample set are true together. These branches are called 'closed' because on them you will find a simple formula (e.g. 'P') and its negation. We know that a formula and its negation cannot both be true together.

Ideally then, we want the tableau to close completely, so *every* branch is a failed attempt to draw a logically possible situation in which the sentences of the counterexample set are true together. In this case we know the counterexample set is inconsistent, so we know the sequent is correct and we know that the argument is valid!

Phew! I hope this brief description hasn't put you off? Like everything else, the best way to learn something is to *do* it. So, let's do a tableau.

Generating Tableaux

Here is the syntactic equivalent of the semantic sequent we tested above:

2) **(P & Q) $\vdash$ ~ Q**

We read this as follows:

"The set consisting of (P & Q) and ~ ~ Q is closed"

Note the addition of a second tilde to '~ Q' .

This argument claim tells us that the tableau we generate from the counterexample of sequent two should be closed.

But it isn't closed. Here is that tableau:

Tableau a)

$$(P \ \& \ Q)$$
$$\sim \sim Q$$

$$Q$$
$$P$$
$$Q$$

You might want to make a copy of tableau a) to refer it as we discuss it.

The first two lines of this tableau represent the counterexample set of sequent two. It lists the premises (the formula on the LHS of the sequent), then the negation of the conclusion (the formula on the RHS of the sequent).

We then write in a gap to distinguish the counterexample set from the tableau it generates. The rest of the tableau is the result of applying the rules of PL. We'll be learning these rules below.

The sentence letter on the first line of the actual tableau is 'Q'. This is the result of applying the 'double negation' rule to '$\sim \sim Q$'. Negation, as we know, reverses the formula on which it operates. As, in this case, it is operating on the formula '$\sim Q$', it has the effect of reversing that. This cancels out the negation, resulting in a simple 'Q'.

The next two sentence letters on the tableau are a 'P', followed in list form by 'Q'. These letters are the result of applying the conjunction rule to (P & Q). We know that (P & Q) is true whenever 'P' is true *and* 'Q' is true. These truth conditions are represented by putting 'P' and 'Q' on the same branch.

In this case there is only one branch to put them on. In more complicated tableaux we would have to put them onto every open branch. We'll see how this works below.

In the case of this tableau, however, putting the 'P' and 'Q' onto the single branch of the tableau completes the tableau. We have applied the rules to all the complex formulae. There is nothing else to do. No contradiction has been generated. The tableau has only one branch and it is *open*.

Discussion

This tableau would be closed if (and only if) a contradiction appeared in it. But there is no contradiction. The tableau demonstrates that the sequent is incorrect. The argument formalised by this sequent is invalid.

To get the counterexample we need we only need to work our way up the open branch(es) listing the sentence letters. In this case the logically possible situation that demonstrates that sequent two is incorrect is: QPQ.

The second 'Q' is irrelevant. It is there because the sentence letter 'Q' appears in more than one formulae of the sequent.

The situation in which 'Q' and 'P' are both true is one in which the premise of the formalised argument is true, yet the conclusion false.

As you'd expect the counterexample is the same as that generated by the truth table by which we tested this argument claim when formalised as a semantic sequent.

Here's the truth table and the tableau together:

	P	Q	(P & Q) $\models$ ~ Q	
1	T	T	$\underline{T}$	x $\underline{F}$
2	T	F	$\underline{F}$	- $\underline{T}$
3	F	T	$\underline{F}$	- $\underline{F}$
4	F	F	$\underline{F}$	- $\underline{T}$
	1	2	3 4 5	6 7 8

(P & Q)
~ ~ Q

Q
P
Q

You'll have noted, I imagine, how much easier it was to generate the tableau than to construct the truth table!

Syntactic Tableaux: How They Work

To create a tableau we work through the counterexample set generated by a sequent.

For each formula we produce, according to the rules of PL, a tree- like representation of its truth-conditions. We add the representation of the second formula onto the bottom of the branches generated by the first formula and so on until we have a tree that is a complete representation of the truth conditions for every formula.

As we work if, in a given branch of the tree, we see a sentence letter '(Q') *and its negation* '(~ Q') we draw a line across that tree and ignore it from then on. That branch is a *failed* attempt to draw a possible situation on which the formulae of the counterexample set are all true together. The truth conditions represented on that branch have generated a contradiction: a situation that is *not* logically possible.

If, having completed our tableau, every branch is closed then *every* attempt to find a logically possible situation in which the formulae of the counterexample set are all true together has failed. The counterexample set is inconsistent. This means, of course, that the sequent is correct and the argument it formalised is *valid*.

Any open branch, however, represents a logically possible situation in which the formulae of the counterexample set are all true together. Only one such branch is needed to show that the counterexample set is consistent , and that the sequent, therefore is incorrect. But there may be more than one branch open. In such a case there is more than one counterexample to the argument that was formalised by means of the sequent.

All we need now is the interpretation to translate the counterexample (s) back into English.

Let's now try a tableau that closes, using the same simple rules we have already met.

A Closed Tableau

Here is another sequent:

3. **(P & Q) ⊢ Q**

There is no counterexample to the third sequent. Here is the tableau generated by its counterexample set:

Tableau b)

(P & Q)
~ Q

P
Q

___

Let's work our way through tableau b) comparing it with tableau a). You might want to copy out both tableaux, the better to refer to them during our discussion. Here again is tableau a):

Tableau a)

(P & Q)
~ ~ Q

Q
P
Q

Discussion

The first two lines of the tableau b) represent the counterexample set of sequent three. In the case of tableau b), however, there is no line equivalent to line three of tableau a). This is because the negated conclusion of sequent three is simply '~ Q' to which no rule need be applied. As in tableau a) the truth conditions of the conjunction (P & Q) are represented, in tableau b), as a list with first 'P', then 'Q'.

But immediately we have a contradiction. The 'Q' that is generated from (P & Q) contradicts the '~ Q' which is the second formula of the counterexample set. Because there is a contradiction in the single branch of tableau b) this tableau is closed.

As there is only one branch in tableau b), and it contains a contradiction, we can be certain that the sequent that generated tableau b) is correct, and the argument it formalises is valid.

Exercise 8.5: Create counterexample sets for the following sequents:

1. $((P \& Q) \vee (P \& \sim Q)) \vdash P$

2. $((R \vee Q), (R \& Q), Q \nvdash \sim R$

3. $\sim R, (Q \vee R), (Q \& P) \vdash P$

Answers on page 400

Exercise 8.6: Do you remember why validity is demonstrated by the *inconsistency* of the counterexample set rather than by its *consistency*?

Answers on page 401

The Rules of Propositional Logic

We are going to look next at more complicated tableaux, those with multiple branches. First, though, we need to learn the syntactic rules of PL. So far we have used only those for double negation and conjunction.

To know the truth table definitions of the truth-functional connectives is to be able to work out most of the rules. You might amuse yourself by trying. A warning though, the conditional, as usual, will probably trip you up – best, probably, just to learn this one (i.e. take it on trust).

Here are the rules with the truth-table definitions. Under each I'll say how we get the former from the latter.

Negation

Negation Truth Table Definition:

P	~P
T	F
F	T

The truth table definition of negation tells us that whenever P is true, the negation of P is false and vice versa.

The Negation Tableau Rule:

The 'double negation' rule tells us that the negation sign negates itself. So if '~~P' is found on a branch, '~P' will be negated, becoming 'P'. The 'stick' in between '~~P' and P, shows that the complex formula does not 'branch' (see below). If there are multiple branches you will have to put the 'stick' and the 'P' onto each open branch.

Conjunction

Conjunction Truth Table Definition:

P	Q	(P & Q)
T	T	T
T	F	F
F	T	F
F	F	F

The truth table for conjunction tells us that (P & Q) is true only when both its conjuncts are true.

Conjunction Tableau Rules

Conjunction Rule	Negated Conjunction Rule
(P & Q)	~(P & Q)

The conjunction rule:
(P & Q)
|
P
Q

The negated conjunction rule:
~(P & Q)
/ \
~P ~Q

The conjunction rule tells us to list the conjuncts onto a single branch. If there are multiple branches the conjuncts must be added to every open branch.

If a conjunction is negated, we need two sticks because there are *two* possible situations in which ~ (P & Q) is true: the situation in which P is false and the situation in which Q is false. These two sticks are called a 'branch'. If it's not the case P *and* Q, then it must be the case that either P is false or Q is false.

Disjunction

Disjunction Truth Table Definition

P	Q	(P ∨ Q)
T	T	T
T	F	T
F	T	T
F	F	F

The truth table for disjunction tells us that (P ∨ Q) is true in every situation except that in which both disjuncts are false.

Disjunction Tableau Rules

Disjunction Rule	Negated Disjunction Rule
(P ∨ Q)	~(P ∨ Q)

Disjunction Rule:
(P ∨ Q)
/ \
P   Q

Negated Disjunction Rule:
~(P ∨ Q)
|
~P
~Q

The disjunction rule breaks the tableau into two branches. There are two possible situations in which (P ∨ Q) is true, the situation in which P is true *and* the situation in which Q is true.

Every undergraduate I have ever taught has asked why there isn't a third branch for the situation in which P *and* Q are true. But that possibility is allowed for in the fact that each branch leaves open the possibility that the other disjunct is true *or* that it is false.

A negated disjunction generates a single branch on which both disjuncts are listed and negated. If it is not the case P *or* Q after all, then P *and* Q will both be false.

Conditional

Conditional Truth Table Definition

P	Q	(P→Q)
T	T	T
T	F	F
F	T	T
F	F	T

The truth table for the conditional says $(P \rightarrow Q)$ is false only if P is true and Q is false. Otherwise it is true.

Conditional Tableau Rules

Conditional Rule	Negated Conditional Rule
(P→Q)	~(P→Q)

The conditional rule is another branching rule. This tells us that again there are two possible situations consistent with the truth of $(P \rightarrow Q)$: the situation in which ~ P is true, and the situation in which Q is true.

A negated conditional is true in just one situation: that in which the antecedent is false *and* the consequent true. This is represented, of course, by listing the negated antecedent, and the un-negated consequent on one branch (and adding this to every open branch of the tableau).

Biconditional

Biconditional Truth Table Definition

P	Q	(P↔Q)
T	T	T
T	F	F
F	T	F
F	F	T

The truth table for the biconditional tells us that (P ↔ Q) is true when both the sentence letters flanking the biconditional are true, or when both are false. If the two differ in truth value the biconditional is false.

The Biconditional Tableau Rule

Biconditional Rule	Negated Biconditional Rule
(P↔Q)	~(P↔Q)

```
Biconditional Rule    Negated Biconditional Rule
     (P↔Q)                    ~(P↔Q)
     /   \                    /    \
   P      ~P               P        ~P
   Q      ~Q              ~Q         Q
```

The biconditional rule is a branching rule. It puts both sentence letters on one branch (so this is a situation in which both are true), and on the other branch the same sentence letters, both negated (showing this is a situation in which both are false)

The negated biconditional is true just in case the two sentence letters do *not* share a truth condition. In one situation one is true the other false, and in the second situation the situation is reversed.

Let's now do a really complicated tableau by generating a tableau for sequent four. We'll do this one together, then you can do a few on your own.

4. $((P \rightarrow Q) \rightarrow (S \;\&\; R)), ((R \lor T) \rightarrow (\sim P \rightarrow \;\sim S)) \vdash P$

Step One: Create the Counterexample Set

To create the counterexample set we list all the formula on the LHS of the sequent, then add the negation of the formula on the RHS of the sequent.

Here's the counterexample set for sequent four:

$$((P \rightarrow Q) \rightarrow (S \;\&\; R))$$
$$((R \lor T) \rightarrow (\sim P \rightarrow \;\sim S))$$
$$\sim P$$

Here we have two complex formulae and one very simple one to which we needn't apply a rule (the '~P').

It doesn't matter in which order you apply the rules. As you gain in experience you will get a feel for which will generate the best tableau (i.e. the one with fewest branches).

Let's start with the first formula listed.

When we apply the rules to a complex formula, we apply them in the order determined by the scope of the truth-functional connectives of that formula.

With truth tables, you may remember, we applied the appropriate rule first to the truth-functional connective with the smallest scope. We worked from the inside out.

When doing tableaux we reverse this order; we work from the outside in. The first rule should be applied to the truth-functor with the *largest* scope.

Step Two: Applying the First Rule

The truth-functional connective with the largest scope in the first formula is the conditional between the two constituent formulae. The other two operators are equal in scope, and both are secondary to this conditional. We can worry about them later.

First, then, we should apply the conditional rule to the first formula:

$$((P \rightarrow Q) \rightarrow (S \ \& \ R))$$
$$((R \lor T) \rightarrow (\sim P \rightarrow \sim S))$$
$$\sim P$$

The conditional rule is a branching rule. So we draw two branches. On the left hand branch we list the negated antecedent of the conditional. On the right hand branch we list the consequent. All we are doing is mindlessly following the conditional rule.

We can now add a tick to the first formula to show that we have provided its truth conditions:

$$((P \rightarrow Q) \rightarrow (S \ \& \ R)) \quad \checkmark$$
$$((R \lor T) \rightarrow (\sim P \rightarrow \sim S))$$
$$\sim P$$

Step Three: Applying the Second Rule

I could now apply the rules to the formulae on the two branches. Instead I am going to move to the second formula so you can see what to do when you have two branches.

The operator with the largest scope in the second formula is again a conditional, that between the two bracketed formulae. The conditional is again (of course) a branching rule, so we have to generate two branches.

But we already have two branches. You might wonder which branch to put the new branches under.

You must put them under *both*. Our aim is to represent the *interaction* between the truth conditions of the formulae, and if there are (at least) two situations in which the first formula are true, and (at least) two situations in which the second formula is true, then there will be four possible situations altogether. That means four branches.

Here is the tableau updated with the result of applying the conditional rule to the second formula. We have also ticked off the second formula to show that it has been done.

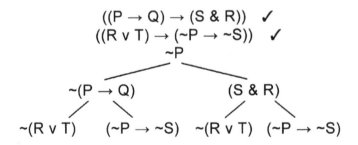

Working On The Branches

We now have four branches, each of them (so far) open. On the left hand side of the tableau we have two branches coming from one complex formula (~ (P →Q)). On the right hand side of the tableau we have another two branches coming from a different complex formula (S & R).

Now we apply the appropriate rule to each of these, putting the result only under the branches containing the formulae to which we are applying the rule.

Remember to tick off the formulae as we apply the rules to them:

$$((P{\rightarrow}Q) \rightarrow (S \ \& \ R)) \checkmark$$
$$((R \ v \ T) \rightarrow ({\sim}P{\rightarrow}{\sim}S)) \checkmark$$
$$\sim P$$

	~(P → Q)✓		(S & R)✓	
~(R v T)		(~P→~S)	~(R v T)	(~P→~S)
P		P	S	S
~Q		~Q	R	R

Check for Contradictions

A glance at the table will tell you that we already have two contradictions. To check for a contradiction , simply start with the formulae at the top and follow down a path. If you find a formula and its negation along the same path, then you will have found a contradiction and thus closed path.

Branches one and two (counting from the left) both contain a 'P' and a '~ P'. We can therefore put a line under each of them to show they are closed.

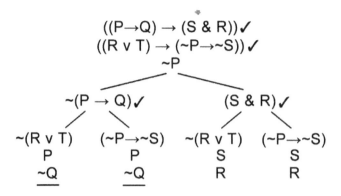

Life will be a little easier now we have only two branches. (We could have had only two branches straight away if I hadn't wanted to show you that you have to put branches under branches!)

Applying The Negated Disjunction Rule to Branch Three

There is one unanalysed formula in each of the two open branches we have left. The one on branch three is a negated disjunction. If we apply this rule we get:

$$((P{\rightarrow}Q) \rightarrow (S \ \& \ R)) ✓$$
$$((R \ v \ T) \rightarrow (\sim P{\rightarrow}\sim S)) ✓$$
$$\sim P$$

$\sim (P \rightarrow Q) ✓$	$(S \ \& \ R) ✓$

$\sim (R \ v \ T) \qquad (\sim P{\rightarrow}\sim S) \qquad \sim (R \ v \ T) ✓ \quad (\sim P{\rightarrow}\sim S)$
$\quad P \qquad\qquad\qquad P \qquad\qquad\quad S \qquad\qquad\qquad S$
$\quad \sim Q \qquad\qquad\quad \sim Q \qquad\qquad\quad R \qquad\qquad\qquad R$
$\qquad\qquad\qquad\qquad\qquad\qquad\qquad\qquad \sim R$
$\qquad\qquad\qquad\qquad\qquad\qquad\qquad\qquad \sim T$

Which immediately gives us another contradiction (an 'R' and a '~ R'). So branch three is closed too, leaving us with only one unticked complex formula (in branch four).

334

Applying the Conditional Rule to the Final Formula in Branch Four

We must be careful about scope in applying rules here. The scope of the negation sign in front of the 'P' is *only* 'P'. That of the negation sign in front of 'S' is *only* 'S'.

This is *not* therefore a negated conditional rule, but only the conditional rule applied to two negations. It is again therefore a branching rule.

Here is the result of applying this rule:

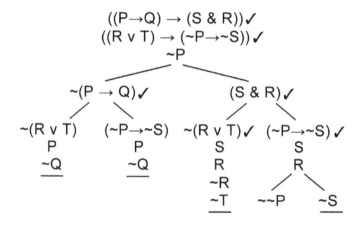

We can already see that branch four will be closed as soon as we apply the double negation rule. Branch five is already closed (because it contains an 'S' and a '~ S').

Here is the final tableau with the double negation rule applied, and branch four closed as well:

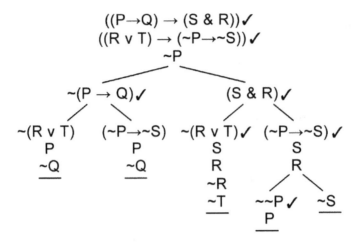

$((P{\to}Q) \to (S \& R))$✓
$((R \lor T) \to ({\sim}P{\to}{\sim}S))$✓
${\sim}P$

${\sim}(P \to Q)$✓ $(S \& R)$✓

${\sim}(R \lor T)$ $({\sim}P{\to}{\sim}S)$ ${\sim}(R \lor T)$✓ $({\sim}P{\to}{\sim}S)$✓
   P   P   S   S
  ${\sim}Q$ ${\sim}Q$ R   R
                                 ${\sim}R$ ${\sim}{\sim}P$✓ ${\sim}S$
                                 ${\sim}T$ P

So, the tableau closes! Sequent four is correct, the counterexample set it generates is closed.

So whichever argument was formalised into this sequent is valid: there is no logically possible situation in which its premises are true and its conclusion false.

Here is a quiz so you can practice constructing tableaux:

Exercise 8.7: Show the following sequents are correct by means of syntactic tableaux:

1. $((~P{\to}Q){\to}Q) \vdash (P{\to}(P{\to}Q))$

2. $(P{\to}(P{\to}Q)) \vdash ((~P{\to}Q){\to}Q)$

Answers on page 402

Here is a final set of exercises for further practice:

Exercise 8.8: Which of the following sequents is correct? Where the sequent is incorrect, give a counterexample.

1.   ~ [P→Q] ⊢ [~P→Q]

2.   ~ [P→Q] ⊢ [P→ ~ Q]

3.   [P→Q] ⊢ ~ [P→ ~ Q]

4.   [P→Q], [R→Q] ⊢ [[P ∨ R] →Q]

5.   [[P→Q] ∨ [R→Q]] ⊢ [[P ∨ R] →Q]

6.   ⊢ [[P→Q] ↔ [~ P→¬Q]]

7.   ⊢ [[P→Q] ↔ [~ Q→¬P]]

8.   [P& ~ P] ⊢ Q

9.   Q ⊢ [P→P]

Answers on page 403

That's it! You can now formalise arguments as sequents of PL, and test them by means of truth tables or syntactic tableaux. Well done!

Let's just reflect on whether you can do everything I said you'd know and be able to do as a result of reading this chapter.

- construct truth tables by which to identify the truth conditions of wffs;

- explain how truth tables work;

- understand how syntactic tableaux correspond to truth table definitions;

- test semantic sequents by means of truth tables;

- test syntactic sequents by means of tableaux;

- understand the impact of a syntactic sequent's being open or closed;

- identify the counterexample for any incorrect sequent.

Well done! You have done extremely well getting to the end of this chapter. You have also got to the end of this book. A serious achievement. I hope you are proud of yourself. You should be. Getting to grips with logic, even at this basic level, takes tenacity and hard work. You have proven yourself capable of both. I hope you have enjoyed the book, and that your reasoning benefits from the work you have done for the rest of your life!

If you have any comments about how I might make changes to the book and help future readers I should be delighted to hear from you. Please email me by means of the contact form on my website www.mariannetalbot.co.uk. You might also like to follow me on twitter (@oxphil_marianne), or Facebook *Marianne Talbot Philosophy*

Good luck!

APPENDIX I

Definitions

Ambiguous: a word or phrase is *ambiguous* if it has more than one meaning.

Structural ambiguity: a *structural ambiguity* is an ambiguity that occurs when the words of a sentence can be grouped together differently.

Lexical ambiguity: A *lexical ambiguity* occurs when one word in a sentence can be understood in different ways.

Cross Referential ambiguity: an *ambiguity of cross reference* occurs when it is unclear to which word a later word refers back.

Argument: an *argument* is a set of sentences in which one sentence is being asserted on the basis of the other(s).

Sound argument: an argument is *sound* iff its premises are all true and its conclusion follows from its premises.

Good argument: an argument is *good* iff its conclusion follows from its premises (irrespective of the truth of its premises).

Valid argument: an argument is *valid* iff there is no logically possible situation in which all its premises are true and its conclusion false.

Invalid argument: an argument is *invalid* iff there is a logically possible situation in which all its premises are true and its conclusion false.

Strong argument: an inductive argument is *strong* iff the truth of all its premises significantly raises the likelihood that its conclusion will be true.

Weak argument: an inductive argument is *weak* iff the truth of all its premises doesn't significantly raise the likelihood that its conclusion will be true.

A priori: to know something *a priori* is to know it without needing to bring to bear any background knowledge of the world.

A posteriori: to know something *a posteriori* is to know it only having brought to bear some background knowledge of the world.

Assertion: an *assertion* is a sentence used with assertoric force to express a belief.

Conclusion: the *conclusion* of an argument is the assertion being made on the basis of the other sentences.

Conjunction: a *conjunction* is a complex sentence formed by means of two simple sentences and the logical word 'and'.

Consistent: a set of sentences is *consistent* iff there is a logically possible situation in which all the sentences in the set can be true together.

> **Inconsistent:** a set of sentences is *inconsistent* iff there is no logically possible situation in which all the sentences in the set can be true together.

Counterexample set: the '*counterexample set*' of an argument is the set of sentences that consists in the premises of the argument plus *the negation of the conclusion of the argument.*

Declarative sentence: a *declarative sentence* is a sentence that could be used with assertoric force to express a belief.

Enthymeme: an *enthymeme* is an argument with a suppressed premise.

Empirically possible: something is *empirically possible* iff it is consistent with the laws of nature as we currently understand them.

Logically possible: something is *logically possible* iff it is consistent with the laws of logic as we currently understand them.

Grue: something is *grue* if it is green and observed or blue and unobserved.

Logical equivalence: two sentences are *logically equivalent* to each other if they are true and false in *exactly* the same conditions.

Monotonic: a property is *monotonic* iff it cannot be changed by the addition of new information.

Non-monotonic: a property is *non-monotonic* iff it can be changed by the addition of new information.

Negation: the *negation* of a sentence is created by tacking 'it is not the case that' on to the front of the sentence.

Premises: *the premise(s)* of an argument are the reason(s) being offered for believing the conclusion.

Proposition: a *proposition* is the content of the belief expressed by a statement.

Semantic sequent: *Semantic sequent* ($\models$): There is no structure in which the formulae on the left hand side are true and the formula on the right hand side false.

Statement: a *statement* is a sentence in use.

Syntactic sequent: *Syntactic Sequent* ($\vdash$): The tableaux generated from the counterexample set of this sequent will close.

Truth conditions: *Truth conditions* are those conditions under which a sentence would be true or false if it were used under normal conditions to express a belief (the strict and literal meaning of a sentence is given by its truth conditions).

Truth-table: a *truth-table* is a tabular representation of a complete set of truth conditions.

Truth value: we attach a *truth value* to a sentence (or the belief it expresses) when we say it is true or we say it is false.

APPENDIX II

Truth Tables

The complete truth table.

P	Q	~P	(P & Q)	(P ∨ Q)	(P→Q)	(P↔Q)
T	T	F	T	T	T	T
T	F		F	T	F	F
F	T	T	F	T	T	F
F	F		F	F	T	T

APPENDIX III

Tableau Rules

The tableau rules:

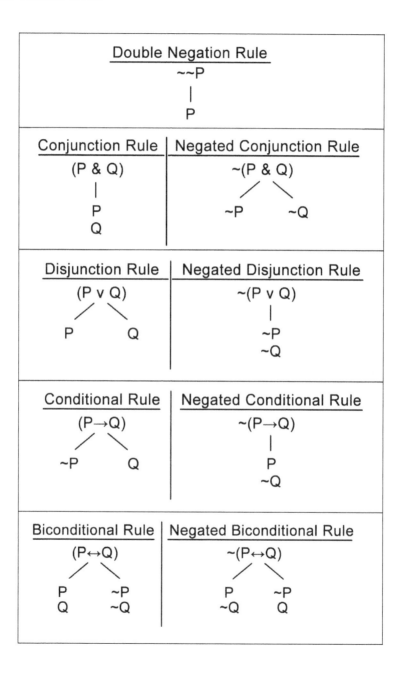

APPENDIX IV

Answers

Answer 1.1

Which of the following sets of sentences are arguments? Remember that a set of sentences is an argument *only* if one sentence is being asserted on the basis of the others.

1. As she got nearer home, her worry increased and she quickened her step. Then, just before she put her key in the front door her mobile rang.

    This is not an argument. It is not being suggested that the increase in her worry, or the quickening of her step, were reasons for believing that her mobile rang. This set of sentences is merely telling us what actually happened.

2. Since Jennifer is the mother of Stan, and Stan is the father of Oliver, Jennifer is the grandmother of Oliver.

    This is an argument.

3. The Challenger exploded because the O-rings failed, and the proper functioning of the O-rings was a necessary part of a safe launch.

    This is an argument.

4. Justin Beiber was late, and many of his fans were upset. The twittersphere was very busy.

    This is not an argument: it is merely being stated that the twittersphere was busy after Justin Beiber was late and upset many of his fans.

5. If the train was held up Jem will be late.

This is a conditional assertion not an argument (similar to 'if she is a professional soprano she will be able to reach top A').

6. The small bird was a robin, the large one a woodpecker.

   This is not an argument, but merely a conjunction of two sentences, with the 'and' left implicit.

7. If the car is not starting you might think about calling the AA.

   This is not an argument but a suggestion.

Answer 1.2

Recognising Declarative Sentences.

1. Is it true that the snow is still falling?

   Yes.

2. Is it true that inflation is slowly rising?

   Yes.

3. Is it true that is it time yet?

   No. This sentence has interrogative, not assertoric, force. It expresses a question not a belief.

4. Is it true that I hereby declare you man and wife?

   Debatable: in use this sentence constitutes the performance of an act of performing a marriage (it is called a 'performative'). If it is a declarative sentence it is a very odd one.

5. Is it true that has the shopping arrived yet?

   No. As (3).

6. Is it true that turn that noise off!?

   No, This sentence has imperative, not assertoric, force. It expresses a command not a belief.

7. Is it true that I hope you feel better?

   Yes.

Answer 1.3

Weak and Strong Meanings:

1. Britain will not have its triple A rating by the end of the year.

2. You are not able to make more money.

3. He is not a millionaire.

Answer 1.4

Recapping Chapter One

1. An argument is a set of sentences in which one sentence is being asserted on the basis of the other(s)

2. The frame test asks whether a sentence can be substituted for '…' in the frame 'Is it true that …?', yielding a grammatical question. If it can then the sentence is a declarative sentence

3. This sentence is not analysable as an argument because neither of its constituent sentences is being asserted on the basis of the other (it is the whole conditional that is being asserted).

4. Interrogative force is used when we want to ask a question. The imperative force is used when we want to issue a command.

5. If we put a sentence in quotation marks we indicate we are talking about that sentence rather than using it.

6. A truth value - true or false – is assigned to a sentence on the basis of whether it we think correctly represents the facts.

7. The parts of a simple sentence are all *sub-sentential*.

8. The weak meaning of a sentence is given by its strict and literal truth conditions.

9. In acting we are guided by our beliefs but motivated by our desires.

10. The Principle of Charity is important because it reminds us that in the appearance of *disagreement* we have evidence for error.

Answer 2.1

1. The only men who can stay here are rich or the only people who can stay here are rich men.

    This is a structural ambiguity.

2. The Headteacher hates children or the Headteacher can't have children.

    A lexical ambiguity

3. The only *people* with whom some women go to the theatre are men who treat them politely, or the only *men* with whom some women will go to the theatre are those who treat them politely, or some women do not go to the theatre, unless with men who treat them politely.

    This is again a structural ambiguity.

4. The student read the essay to the tutor and he (the student) was bored by it or the student read the essay to the tutor and he (the tutor) was bored by it.

    An ambiguity of cross reference.

5. Children that are irritating should be banned or the activity of irritating children should be banned.

    Another structural ambiguity.

6. The only man who doesn't admire *James's* mother is James or every man admires *his own mother* except James.

    Yet another structural ambiguity.

7. He saw the duck that belonged to her or he saw her try to avoid a missile by ducking.

   A lexical ambiguity.

Answer 2.2

Identifying Conclusions

1. The conclusion is 'he deserved to be sent off' (as indicated by the word 'so').

2. The conclusion is 'women are less intelligent than men' (as indicated by the word 'therefore').

3. The conclusion is 'The butler couldn't have done it'.

4. The conclusion is 'The green movement is wrong to think we should recycle paper'.

Answer 2.3

'And' Conjoining Predicates or Sentences

1. Yes. 'They visited Cairo' and 'They visited Luxor.'

2. No, this cannot be analysed as 'the dress was blue *and* the dress was green', the 'and' links two predicates.

3. Yes. 'He was clever.' and 'His twin was clever.' (ideally we'd remove the cross-reference by supplying his name, so the two sentences would be independent of each other).

Answer 2.4

Identifying Premises

1. The premise is 'he committed a serious foul'.

2. The premise is 'women's brains are on average smaller than men's'.

3. The premises are 'The butler was in the pantry' and 'The Count was in his study' (note that I have split apart a conjoined sentence, and that 'after all' is a premise indicator.).

4. The premises are 'Paper comes from trees which are renewable' and 'Recycling paper has been abandoned in many American cities because it is too expensive'.

Answer 2.5

Eliminating Cross References

Can you eliminate the cross references from our target argument?

NOTE: There might not be a cross-reference in which case you shouldn't add anything.

Premise one: There is no cross reference to eliminate here

Premise two: There is no cross reference to eliminate here

Premise three: Certainly, if the economy flourishes, **the German** Government will survive

Premise four: There is no cross reference to eliminate here

Premise five: Unless **Herr Kohl** gets **grass roots support**, **the German** Government will only last in a flourishing economy

Conclusion: There is no cross reference to eliminate here.

Answer 2.6

Eliminating Irrelevancies

Premise one: The snowdrops don't come out until spring

Premise two: The snowdrops are out

Conclusion: It is spring.

   You might think that this argument is hardly the point of the passage above. I think you are right. We do *so* many more things with language than offer arguments. But your current task, given that you are reading this book, is to pick out, from everything else, the argument being offered.

Answer 2.7

Eliminating Inconsistent Terminology

Premise one: The economy is not flourishing

Premise two: Herr Kohl is humiliated

Premise three: Herr Kohl will not get grass roots support if Herr Kohl is humiliated

Premise four: Unless Herr Kohl gets grass roots support, The German Government will only last in a flourishing economy

Conclusion: The German Government won't last the year.

Note: don't be worried about the fact I have changed premise two from 'Herr Kohl is *about to be* humiliated' to 'Herr Kohl *is* humiliated'. I have done this because premise three has, as a constituent sentence, 'Herr Kohl *is* humiliated'. I have judged that my change doesn't change the meaning of premise two in any way that affects the argument, except in making it clearer that premises two and three share a constituent sentence.

Answer 2.8

Identifying Suppressed Premises

1. The suppressed premise is: 'Anyone committing a serious foul deserves to be sent off'.

   This is not controversial.

2. The suppressed premise is: 'The size of the brain determines the intelligence of the owner of the brain'.

   This is controversial.

3. The suppressed premise is: 'The butler couldn't have been in the pantry *and* in the study'.

   This is not controversial.

4. The suppressed premises are: 'If a resource is renewable we needn't recycle goods made with it' and 'If something is too expensive it should be abandoned'.

   Both these premises are potentially controversial.

Answer 2.9

Analysing Simple Arguments

1.

Premise one: The dog only ever barks when it sees a stranger

Premise two: The dog is barking

Conclusion: The dog can see a stranger.

2.

Premise one: Mungo likes the Big Bang Theory

Premise two: Joanna likes to watch the News

Premise three: The Big Bang Theory and the News are both on at 6pm

Conclusion: Mungo and Joanna will have to buy another television or agree to compromise.

3.

Premise one: The car started to make a strange noise.

Premise two: (suppressed) Having strange noises checked out costs money.

Conclusion: If having this strange noise checked out is going to cost me money, I shall have to economise.

Answer 3.1

Are the arguments sound, good, neither or unknown?

1. The argument is sound.

2. The argument is not good (it 'affirms the consequent').

3. Good but not sound.

4. Neither good nor sound.

Answer 3.2

Please say whether the following situations are logically possible, impossible or necessary, or empirically impossible, possible or necessary, or such that we can't tell:

1. Logically possible.

2. Empirically impossible, but logically possible.

3. Logically impossible.

4. Logically impossible.

5. Logically necessary.

6. We don't know.

7. Empirically, but not logically, necessary.

8. Empirically impossible. We don't know whether this is logically impossible.

Answer 3.3

**Please say whether the following arguments are
valid, invalid, strong or weak:**

1. Valid.

2. Strong (ish). The cat might be very old or have some
   illness.

3. Invalid (another case of affirming the consequent).

4. Weak.

Answer 3.4

**Might the addition of further information change
our minds about an evaluation of the following
arguments:**

1. This is a valid argument nothing could change this fact.

2. This seems fairly strong unless we learn something about
   Tom that suggests he is in the 10% of oilmen who are not
   rich.

3. This seems a reasonably good argument. But if we learn
   that Jaz doesn't do any work, or that she recently had an
   accident that left her brain-damaged, we might change our
   minds.

Answer 3.5

Can you evaluate this as a good or bad argument despite the fact you have no idea what it is talking about?

This argument is an argument of the form *modus tollens* or *modus tollendo tollens* (in Latin 'the way that denies by denying). Informally it is called 'denying the consequent'. Any argument of this form is a *good* deductive argument.

Answer 3.6

Are the following arguments inductive or deductive?

Argument 1 is inductive. On the following interpretation...

P: Thousands of babies born with T21 have DS and that no baby born with T21 does not have DS

Q   The next baby born with T21 will therefore have DS

...its structure is revealed to be:

Premise one: P

Conclusion: Q.

This argument cannot be evaluated a priori. Nor is it conclusive. Logic would permit the birth of a baby with T21 and not DS. This argument is strong, but it is not valid.

Argument 2 is deductive. On the following interpretation:

P: Thousands of babies born with T21 have DS, and no babies with T21 have *not* had DS

Q: There is a causal law relating T21 and DS

R: T21 necessitates DS

S: It is not possible that a child should be born with T21 but *not* DS

its structure is revealed to be:

Premise one: If P then Q

Premise two: If Q then R

Premise three: If R then S

Conclusion: If P then S.

This *can* be evaluated a priori. In the next chapter we shall see that this argument is valid, and therefore conclusively so.

Answer 3.7

Please identify all the following arguments as either deductive or inductive.

1. Deductive

2. Inductive.

3. Deductive.

4. Inductive.

5. Inductive.

6. Inductive

Answer 4.1

**Can you work out, from the definition of validity ,
why circular arguments (arguments the
conclusions of which are amongst their premises)
are valid but not persuasive?**

If the premises of a circular argument are true its conclusion
must be true. The conclusion *is* a premise. We will only be
persuaded of the conclusion if we *already* believed the premise.
We will discuss this in chapter five.

Answer 4.2

**Why should a population's being *small* mean that a
sample must be a reasonable percentage of it to be
large enough?**

A sample of 5% of a population of 100 (5) will not rule out
distortions due to chance. 5% of a population of 100,000
(5,000) will.

Answer 4.3

"Drugs! Everyone does them, but which ones do you do?"

Those who don't take drugs are probably less likely to respond to this invitation, so the sample will be biased towards those who do take drugs.

Answer 4.4

Evaluate the following inductive generalisations.

1. The sample is unrepresentative (in the UK at least)

2. It would be important to know the source of the information offered in the premise. We need also to know how the key terms are being defined. Might this be a deductive argument with the premise 'positive results are more likely to be unreliable' suppressed?

3. The conclusion is too strong to be supported by these premises. 'James has a chance of winning the Open' is better.

4. This generalisation takes us implicitly from a particular disaster (the terrorist attack) to the belief that it is dangerous to use the Tube (the London Underground). The conclusion is unjustified. There are many more journeys by Tube that have been concluded safely than ones that have led to involvement in a terror attack (or any other disaster).

Answer 4.5

Evaluate the following abductive argument.

If science cannot explain the nature of values, if we *need* an explanation of the nature of values, and if it is *only* appeal to God that will explain the nature of values, then the argument is a good one. These are big 'ifs'.

Answer 4.6

What do you think of this analogy?

Answer: It is one thing for an individual to exercise his will in suppressing his emotions as guided by reason. It is another for a state to use its soldiers to suppress part of the population for the greater good of another part. You might like to read about Plato's analogy here: http://www.iep.utm.edu/ republic /

Answer 4.7

Is the following an argument from analogy or authority? Is it a strong argument?

It is an argument from analogy , but can be used as an argument from authority.

Feynmann was a physicist, rather than a philosopher of science. *As a physicist,* Feynmann can be thought of as an authority on the usefulness, to scientists, of philosophy of science. It is worth examining his argument, therefore, *as an analogy* (as well as an argument from authority.

Ornithologists tell us what birds need to flourish so we can provide it. Arguably, therefore, ornithology *is* useful to birds. *Knowledge of* ornithology is not. Birds cannot reflect on themselves, their needs and their actions and learn from such reflection. Scientists, of course, can. Philosophy of science is clearly not a necessary condition for being a successful scientist. But this does not entail that philosophy of science is of no use to scientists.

Answer 5.1

Must we reject the conclusion of an invalid argument?

No. If an argument is invalid it tells us *nothing* about the truth of its conclusion. We shouldn't accept the conclusion on the basis of the argument. But there might be other good reasons for accepting it.

Answer 5.2

If the conclusion of a valid argument can be false, why is validity so useful?

It is useful because it can reveal truths only implicit in the premises (as in the 'Romeo' argument of chapter three on page 100) and because it is truth-preserving. If we know that an argument is valid, but that its conclusion is false, we know that at least one of its premises is false. This can be very useful. It is also, of course, useful because if we know the premises are true we know the conclusion *must* be true.

Answer 5.3

Could deductive arguments with the following *actual* truth values be valid or not?

1.   Yes.

2.   Yes.

3.   No.

4.   Yes.

5.   Yes.

Answer 5.4

I have just told you why arguments 5.9 and 5.10 are valid, but can you say more?

Argument 5.9 is such that there is no possible situation in which its premise is true and its conclusion false because there is *no possible situation in which its conclusion is false* (so how *could* there be a possible situation in which its premise is true *and* its conclusion false?).

Argument 5.10 is such that there is no possible situation in which its premise is true and its conclusion false because there is *no possible situation in which its premise is true* (so how *could* there be a possible situation in which its premise is true *and* its conclusion false?).

Answer 5.5

Please provide counterexample sets for these deductive arguments.

Counterexample set

One:

If Lee is a Chinese Spy then Lee speaks Chinese.

Lee speaks Chinese.

It is not the case that Lee is a Chinese Spy.

Two:

If Gemma was in the taxi last night then Gemma stole my purse.

Gemma was in the taxi last night.

It is not the case that Gemma stole my purse.

Three:

Peter is an accountant or James is an accountant.

Peter is not an accountant.

It is not the case that James is an accountant.

Answer 5.6

Providing an interpretation please strip the content from the counterexample set of argument 5.12.

On the following interpretation:

P: Thousands of babies born with T21 have DS and no baby born with T21 does not have DS

Q: There is a causal law relating T21 and DS

R: T21 necessitates DS

S: It is not possible that a baby should be born with T21 but *not* DS

This is the bare structure of the counterexample set for argument 5.12:

If P then Q.

If Q then R.

If R then S.

It is not the case that if P then S.

Answer 5.7

Providing an interpretation, please strip the counterexample sets below of their content, then decide whether they are consistent or not

Interpretation	Counterexample set	Consistent?
P: Lee is a Chinese spy Q: Lee speaks Chinese	If P then Q Q Not-P	Yes

P: Gemma was in the
    taxi last night
Q: Gemma stole my
    purse
	If P then Q
	P
	Not- Q
		No

P: Peter is an accountant Q: James is an accountant	P or Q Not-P Not-Q	No

Answer 5.8

Please decide, with respect to each of the arguments above, whether it is valid. If it is not valid please provide a counterexample.

Interpretation	Counterexample	Consistent?	Valid?
P: Lee is a Chinese Spy Q: Lee speaks Chinese	If P then Q Q Not-P	Yes	No
P: Gemma was in the taxi last night Q: Gemma stole my purse	If P then Q P Not-Q	No	Yes
P: Peter is an accountant Q: James is an accountant	P or Q Not-P Not-Q	No	Yes

The counterexample for the first is:

Lee speaks Chinese

Lee isn't a Chinese spy

The other two counterexample sets are not consistent so do not have counterexamples

Answer 5.9

Do you think that the premises of argument 5.12 are true?

Premise one seems to assume that where there is correlation there is causation. We saw in chapter four (page 153) that this is not always correct. Premise one, therefore, might be false.

Premise two seems to assume that causation is invariably deterministic. Again we saw in chapter four (page 158) that this is not the case. Premise two, therefore, might be false.

Premise three is true, at least on one understanding of 'necessitates': if A *necessitates* B then A cannot occur without B. The relevant sense of 'necessitates' is, of course, *empirical* necessitation.

The first two premises might both be false, or one or other of them might be false. The validity of argument 5.12 does not, therefore, *guarantee* the truth of its conclusion. The conclusion might be true or it might be false.

Answer 5.10

If an argument is valid and its conclusion false, we know for certain that at least one of its premises must be false.

Answer 5.11

You might like to go through argument 5.12 adding 'empirically'where relevant.

Premise one: If thousands of babies born with T21 have DS and no baby born with T21 does not have DS, then there is a causal law relating T21 and DS

Premise two: If there is a causal law relating T21 and DS then T21 **empirically** *necessitates* DS

Premise three: If T21 **empirically** *necessitates* DS then it is not **empirically** possible that a baby should be born with T21 but *not* DS

Conclusion: If thousands of babies born with T21 have DS and no baby born with T21 does not have DS then it is not **empirically** possible that a baby should be born with T21 but *not* DS.

Answer 6.1

Is this a fallacy?

No, it is an *instance* of a fallacy. You might also say that it is an instance of fallacious reasoning. It is an instance of the fallacy of *hasty generalisation* (and perhaps *post hoc ergo propter hoc*). The fallacy is the argument *type* not the argument *token*.

Answer 6.3

Please decide which of the following arguments is a case of affirming the consequent, and which is a valid instance of modus ponens:

1.   An instance of affirming the consequent.

2.   An instance of modus ponens.

3.   An instance of modus ponens.

4.   An instance of affirming the consequent.

5.   An instance of modus ponens.

6.   An instance of affirming the consequent.

Answer 6.4

Anyone familiar with Daniel Kahneman's book Thinking, Fast and Slow will see that the following thought experiment is modelled on his 'Linda' and 'Tom W' thought experiments.

The probability of Jane studying humanities is higher than the probability that she is studying dance. This is because there are so many more students studying humanities subjects than there are studying dance.

If you thought otherwise you might have been misled by the independent information that Jane likes to watch dancing and that she likes to dance herself. But this tells you that *if* Jane is studying humanities she is more likely to be studying dance than philosophy. It does not make it *more probable* that she is studying dance than that she is studying humanities.

Answer 6.5

What is the problem that should cause us to hesitate in formalising this argument in the manner suggested?

Criminal actions are indeed illegal if 'criminal action' is understood as the action *of* a criminal. Murder trials are indeed criminal actions, when 'criminal action' is understood as action *against* a criminal. The validity of this argument turns on the words 'criminal action' meaning the same thing in premises one and two. As they do not mean the same thing in premises one and two the argument is not valid.

Answer 7.1

Is argument 5.13 from chapter five an argument the validity of which turns solely on its propositional structure?

No it isn't. If we were formalising this argument we would have to use the language of *predicate logic*. Premise two in particular tells us that all arguments that satisfy one predicate (being such that if their premises are true their conclusions are also true), also satisfy another (they are valid).

I said in chapter five that this argument couldn't be formalised by means of sentence letters. This is one reason why. We shall look at another later in chapter seven.

Answer 7.2

**Can you say which of these sentence connectives is
truth functional and give complete, partial or
blank truth-tables as appropriate?**

1.   Yes:

P	Q	P or Q
T	T	T
T	F	T
F	T	T
F	F	F

You might have put 'F' into the first row of this truth-table. This
is because the English 'or' is ambiguous; it can be inclusive (as
I have shown it) or exclusive (as you have it). In the first case it
includes 'or both', in the second case it doesn't.

2.   No:

P	Q	P because Q
T	T	?
T	F	F
F	T	?
F	F	?

If P is true and Q false, then P can't be the cause of Q, so 'P because Q' must be false. But we have no idea whether 'P because Q' is true in any other situation. To know that we'd have to know more than the truth value of the constituent sentences; we'd also have to know whether the state of affairs described by P is causally related to the state of affairs described by Q. This means we'd have to know the *meanings* of 'P' and 'Q' not just their truth value.

Note: In my answer to this I am thinking of this 'because' as talking about *causes* not *reasons*. But consider 'the cheque is invalid because it is filled in incorrectly'. Here 'because' appeals to a reason rather than a cause. My explanation, though, would also apply to this. I mention it, therefore, to avoid confusion. I owe this point to Dr. Paula Boddington of Oxford University.

3.   Yes:

P	It is not the case that P
T	F
F	T

4.   No:

P	It is necessarily the case that P
T	?
T	F

Even if 'P' is true we have no idea whether it is *necessarily* true. It might be *contingently* true. If P is false, though, we know that 'it is necessarily the case that P' *must* be false. No falsehood is necessarily true.

Answer 7.3

Provide an interpretation and substitute the appropriate sentence letters for the sentences of the target argument.

P: The economy is flourishing

Q: Herr Kohl is humiliated

R: Herr Kohl will get grass roots support

S: The German Government will last.

Premise one: It is not the case that P

Premise two: Q

Premise three: If Q then it is not the case that R

Premise four: Unless R, S only if P

Conclusion: It is not the case that S.

You will note that I have allocated 'P' to the sentence 'the economy is flourishing'. This means that we have to use *'it is not the case that P'* to represent premise one.

Answer 7.4

The following partially formalised sentence: 'Unless R, S only if P' was the result of applying an interpretation to the sentence: "Unless Herr Kohl gets grass roots support, the German Government will only last if the economy flourishes". Can you put brackets into the formalisation to show the scope of the truth functional connectives?

(Unless R (S only if P)).

Answer 7.5

Can you add brackets to show the ambiguity of the following strings?

1. ((P and R) or S) or (P and (R or S)).

2. ((If P then R) or S) or (If P then (R or S)).

3. Not (P and Q) or (not-P and Q).

4. ((If P then not R) or S) or (If P then not (R or S)).

Answer 7.6

**Translate the following sentences as negations,
drawing attention to infelicities in translation**

1. ~ children will be allowed.

2. ~ I am beating my dog (we lose the implication that I *was* beating my dog).

3. ~ she performed well.

4. ~ Pegasus exists.

5. ~ there is someone at home.

6. ~ he'll get in (we lose the emphasis of 'never').

Answer 7.7

Translate the following sentences, where possible, as conjunctions, drawing attention to infelicities in translation.

If the conjunction can't be used say why.

1. (Jane was happy & Jane was exhausted). We lose the implication that this is unusual.

2. (The tick was there & the tick was faint).

3. This cannot be translated by means of the conjunction without losing the implication that they are each other's twin. This implication is too important to lose.

4. This probably cannot be translated by means of '&' because the 'who was looking tired' seems to identify the student under discussion, rather than giving us additional information. If it had commas around 'who was looking tired' this probably could be translated with'&'..

5. (The book was the course textbook & the book was very long).

6. (Your suggestion is incorrect & your suggestion is outrageous).

7. (Headington is a suburb of Oxford & Cumnor is a suburb of Oxford).

8. This cannot be translated by means of the conjunction. 'Headington is five miles apart & Cumnor is five miles apart' makes no sense.

Answer 7.8

Translate the following sentences by means of the vel

1. (James is coming with Anna ∨ James will be late).

2. (We must impose austerity ∨ we'll never reduce the national debt).

3. (We'll go to the festival ∨ the weather is foul).

4. (Jane is coming, ∨ John will opt out).

Answer 7.9

Translate the following sentences by means of the arrow drawing attention to any infelicities in translation

1. (he has trained properly → he should win).

2. (one more student fails to hand in their work → I'll explode).

3. (The paper turns red → the liquid is acidic) Note that the liquid's being acidic is *necessary* for the paper's turning red. Note also the need to modify the grammar of the antecedent clause.

4. (if the sun is out → we'll have a picnic) Note again the modification of the grammar.

5. (he is right → I will get the sack).

Answer 7.10

**Translate the following sentences by means of the
biconditional drawing attention to any infelicities
in translation**

1. (You can enter the competition ↔ you are eligible).

2. (He will become a doctor ↔ his thesis passes).

3. (He slays the dragon ↔ he marries the princess).

   We are assuming the Princess has no choice but to marry
   the man who slays the dragon. – I owe this example to Dr.
   Paula Boddington.

Answer 7.11

**Using the truth functor symbols of PL and the
interpretation provided, please translate the
following premises and conclusion into the
language of PL:**

Premise one: ~ P

Premise two: Q

Premise three: (Q → ~ R)

Premise four: (R ∨ (S → P))

Conclusion: ~ S.

Answer 7.12

Can you supply the syntactic sequents that correspond to the semantic sequents above, and explain their meaning?

$\vdash (P \lor \sim P)$ or 'the set consisting in $\sim (P \lor \sim P)$ is closed'.

$(P \mathbin{\&} \sim P) \vdash$ or 'the set consisting in $(P \mathbin{\&} \sim P)$ is closed'.

Answer 7.13

Which of the following English sentences can be translated into a formula of PL containing at least one truth functional connective? If a sentence can't be so translated, please say why. If it can be translated, please translate it.

1. No, because although 'Marianne is wearing jeans' is a simple sentence, the 'I know that' cannot be translated by any symbol of PL. 'I know that P' is not truth-functional.

2. Yes; this can be translated as a negation. It will become '~ P'.

3. Yes, this can be translated as a disjunction. It will become (P ∨ Q).

4. No, although this complex sentence is partly constituted of a simple sentence, the 'It is hard to say that' cannot be translated by any symbol of PL. It is not truth-functional.

5. Yes; this can be translated as a conditional. It will become (P → Q).

Answer 8.1

Please order the truth-functional connectives in the following formulae from that with the smallest scope to that with the largest scope.

1. Smallest: negation, largest: conditional.

2. Smallest: disjunction., largest: negation.

3. Smallest: negation, largest: disjunction.

4. Smallest: negation, next smallest: conjunction, largest: conditional.

5. Smallest: disjunction, largest: biconditional.

Please provide complete truth tables for the following wffs, indicating which column gives us the truth value for the whole wff by using upper case, underlined, truth values.

I have put in only the truth values for the truth-functional connectives so the tables are not cluttered.

P	Q	(P→~Q)		~(P v Q)		(P v ~Q)	
T	T	**F**	f	**F**	t	**T**	f
T	F	**T**	t	**F**	t	**T**	t
F	T	**T**	f	**F**	t	**F**	f
F	F	**T**	t	**T**	f	**T**	t

R	P	Q	(R→(P & ~Q))			((P v R) ↔ Q)	
T	T	T	**F**	f	f	t	**T**
T	T	F	**T**	t	t	t	**F**
T	F	T	**F**	f	f	t	**T**
T	F	F	**F**	f	t	t	**F**
F	T	T	**T**	f	f	t	**T**
F	T	F	**T**	t	t	t	**F**
F	F	T	**T**	f	f	f	**F**
F	F	F	**T**	f	t	f	**T**

Answer 8.3

If all the rows under a sequent are blank (so the sequent is not incorrect) is the argument valid or invalid?

It is valid – the lack of a cross means that there is no logically possible situation in which all the premises of the argument are true *and* the conclusion false.

Answer 8.4

**Test the following semantic sequents by means of
truth tables, giving counterexamples where
possible.**

1.

R	P	Q	(P v Q), P ⊧ (R & Q)
T	T	T	T̲ T̲ ✓ T̲
T	T	F	T̲ T̲ x F̲
T	F	T	T̲ F̲ - T̲
T	F	F	F̲ F̲ - F̲
F	T	T	T̲ T̲ x F̲
F	T	F	T̲ T̲ x F̲
F	F	T	T̲ F̲ - F̲
F	F	F	F̲ F̲ - F̲

(P ∨ Q), P ⊧ (R & Q) is invalid. It has 3 counterexamples: the
situation in which R and P are true but Q is false, the situation
in which R is false, whilst P and Q are both true, and the
situation in which P is true but R and Q both false.

Answer 8.4 contd

2.

R	P	Q	(P→Q) ⊨ (P→(Q & R))		
T	T	T	T	✓	T
T	T	F	F	-	F
T	F	T	T	✓	T
T	F	F	T	✓	T
F	T	T	T	x	F
F	T	F	F	-	F
F	F	T	T	✓	T
F	F	F	T	✓	T

(P→Q) ⊨ (P→(Q & R)) is also invalid. It has only one counterexample: the situation in which P and Q but R is false.

3.

R	P	Q	$(P{\to}R)$, $(R{\to}Q) \models (P{\to}R)$
T	T	T	T̲ T̲ ✓ T̲
T	T	F	T̲ F̲ - T̲
T	F	T	T̲ T̲ ✓ T̲
T	F	F	T̲ F̲ - T̲
F	T	T	F̲ T̲ - F̲
F	T	F	F̲ T̲ - F̲
F	F	T	T̲ T̲ ✓ T̲
F	F	F	T̲ T̲ ✓ T̲

$(P{\to}R)$, $(R{\to}Q) \models (P{\to}R)$ is valid. There is no logically possible situation in which its premises are true and its conclusion false. Every situation in which its premises are all true is also a situation in which its conclusion is true. Congratulations if you noticed that this is a circular argument.

Answer 8.4 contd

4.

P	(P & ~ P) ⊨
T	<u>F</u> f
F	<u>F</u> t

(P & ~ P) ⊨ is valid, it shows that the formula is a contradiction (it is false in every logically possible situation).

5.

P	⊨ (P v ~ P)
T	<u>T</u> f
F	<u>T</u> t

⊨ (P ∨ ~ P) is valid, it shows that the formula is a tautology (it is true in every logically possible situation).

Answer 8.5

Create counterexample sets for the following sequents:

1.

((P & Q) ∨ (P & ~ Q))

~ P

2.

((R ∨ Q) (R & Q) Q

~ ~ R

3.

~ R

(Q ∨ R) (Q & P)

~ P

Answer 8.6

Do you remember why validity is demonstrated by the *inconsistency* of the counterexample set rather than by its *consistency*

Answer: An argument is valid iff there is no logically possible situation in which all its premises are true and its conclusion false. In creating the counterexample set we are describing just such a situation. If the sentences of the counterexample set *can* all be true together (if the counterexample set is *consistent*) then *there is* a logically possible situation in which the premises are all true and the conclusion false. If the counterexample set is inconsistent this demonstrates that there is no logically possible situation in which all the premises are true and yet the conclusion false. The argument is therefore valid.

Answer 8.7

**Show the following sequents are correct by means
of syntactic tableaux:**

1.

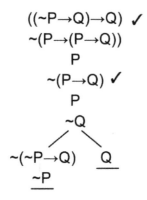

2.

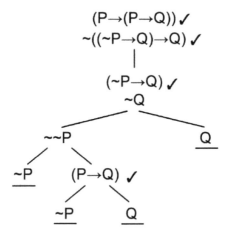

Answer 8.8

Which of the following sequents is correct? Where the sequent is incorrect, give a counterexample.

1. Correct.

2. Correct.

3. Incorrect. Counterexample: P is false and Q is true, and P is false and Q is false.

4. Correct.

5. Incorrect. Counterexamples: P is true, Q is false, R is false, and P is false, Q is false, R is true.

6. Incorrect. Counterexamples: P is false and Q is true, and P is true and Q is false.

7. Correct.

8. Correct.

9. Correct.

INDEX

definition, 256
    rows and possible situations,
        297–98
Uranus, 141
utterance tone of, 33–35
validity

definition, 92, 177–82
    of 'invalid', 92
well-formed formulae (wffs), 247,
    266
Wood, Chris, 3, 9

CPSIA information can be obtained
at www.ICGtesting.com
Printed in the USA
LVHW011545131221
706074LV00009B/955